FAMILY BOATING

Family Boating

A Guide to Successful Family Cruising

JUDY and JIM ANDREWS

Illustrations by Jim Andrews

HOLLIS & CARTER
THE BODLEY HEAD
LONDON SYDNEY
TORONTO

British Library Cataloguing
in Publication Data
Andrews, Judy
Family boating
1. Yachts and yachting.
I. Title   II. Andrews, Jim
797.1'24   GV813
ISBN 0-370-30407-1
0-370-30473-X PbK

©Judy and Jim Andrews 1982
Printed in Great Britain for
Hollis & Carter
an associate company of
The Bodley Head Ltd
9 Bow Street, London WC2E 7AL
by Redwood Burn Ltd.
Trowbridge, Wiltshire
Set in Baskerville
*First published as a paperback and
simultaneously as a hard-cover edition 1982*

CONTENTS

LIST OF PLATES
(Between pages 80 and 81)

All photographs from authors' collection.

WITH THANKS TO OUR DAUGHTERS
and to the wisdom and advice of many boating
parents and friends, and to tips gleaned from
Yachting Monthly and *Practical Boat Owner* over the
years. Numerous helpful ideas were kindly
contributed by Denny Desoutter and Guido
Waldman of Hollis & Carter, as well as by Michael
Horniman of A.P. Watt Ltd. For all of this, and to
all from whom we learnt to make our own family
boating fun, we are sincerely grateful.

Judy and Jim Andrews,
Kippford, 1981.

I

Families in Boats

The gently burbling carrycot waiting amidst the pile of assorted gear we were about to ferry out to our ketch caused raised eyebrows all round. Friends and relatives (and a few total strangers) stared, apparently aghast – then looked from it to us.

'You don't think it's a bit *soon*?' someone enquired, tentatively. 'I mean, if anything was to happen to the boat . . .'

And a few years later, when we had a total of three daughters below the age of four milling around as we prepared to go sailing, there were frequent appalled cries of 'What if they should fall overboard?' and 'Do you think it's *wise* to put to sea when they're only *that* age?'

To be honest, we think it was wise enough, for we took care that nothing did happen, either to the boat or to our children, and the latter have now safely grown up with a knowledge of and respect for the sea, and a joyful appreciation of its creatures, coastlines, and the art of sailing.

We never did feel that, as infants, they were 'too young' for the sport, nor were we 'terrified they might fall overboard' as some people thought we should be, because we did much thinking in advance, and worked out ways of preventing any such mishaps. We made some pretty awful mistakes, of course – but they taught us lessons, and provided answers to be acted upon.

On the other hand, there were so many occasions when we were impressed by the clear enjoyment of a family all pulling together to make a cruise a real pleasure. There was that sunlit evening, for instance, when our three toddlers were sharing their second cruise together among the sea-lochs of the Firth of Clyde. After a lively day ashore and afloat, which had left adults and children happily tired, we put in to our night's anchorage. It was a charming spot, and we were the only boat in, lying on our own reflection in the middle of a small, silent pool below a steep, tree-clad mountainside. Wild rhododendron foliage, loaded with pink blossoms, cascaded down the rocks to the water's edge.

When the children were tucked up in bed and the adults were relaxing with a drink and discussing the next day's plans, the utter stillness of that lovely place was softly broken by an approaching chuckle of water under the bows of what turned out to be a chunky, modest-sized cruiser. We saw her masthead first, over the rocky point, then the rest of her came bustling in through the narrow entrance under sail. She looked thoroughly business-like, with neat paintwork, tidy gear, and a dinghy in davits at the stern, and she was crewed by a family of four.

Slowly her bow-wave died as she lost the wind in the lee of the trees, but unlike what one might expect of so many yachts nowadays, there was no sudden roar of an engine to destroy the peace. Her skipper knelt at the bow, preparing the anchor and occasionally pointing out to his wife, back in the cockpit, the place he had selected. She, a cheerful, comfortable-looking woman, was steering with a relaxed, easy manner, while two girls aged about eight and ten at a guess, stood by the halyards at the foot of the mast.

Rounding expertly into what was left of the breeze, the yacht drifted to a halt, sails fluttered down, and the anchor went over with a splash and a rumble of chain – all with hardly a word being spoken. In moments, father and daughters were busy on the cabintop, stowing the mains'l and chattering about the surroundings, while the mother had disappeared below to get the supper going.

There was no rush about their movements, yet it seemed to us only a few more seconds before all was secured and similarly the davit falls were being smartly manned by the two girls. The dinghy was deftly launched, and with lifejackets tied on, they dropped into the little boat, took an oar apiece, and went rowing off to explore the anchorage. It was obviously a very familiar routine for them.

For the two of us, sitting clutching our drinks, lost in admiration, it had been a joy to watch, and a most encouraging experience too, when we turned our minds towards the years lying ahead of our own family.

What to avoid

Alas, as we knew only too well from several saddened boat-minded parents, the sort of scene we had just witnessed was by no means always typical. We have too often chatted to couples who cruised alone, and discovered that yes, they also had youngsters – who were 'staying with their granny, you know, because they don't really like cruising'. Sooner or later, out would come the tale of the time when the kids were with them, but it had got a bit rough and wee Fiona was seasick, and young Colin had got trodden on by Father when the boy had 'stupidly' got in the way during a rather wild gybe. One was left to guess that the poor little chap maybe hadn't much enjoyed being shouted at either, when he was hurt and frightened to start with. No doubt to be fair, in the heat of such a fraught moment, the father probably hadn't had much time for niceties, but the result impressed on a youngster's mind would be more or less inevitable; from then on, 'going in the boat' would be a thing to avoid. It is all too easy to suggest afterwards that such parents might have done better to sail their boat less hard when their young were on board, so avoiding sudden difficulties; but there, it's easy to be wise . . .

The most extreme case of actual mutiny in a family's lower decks which we ever came across was one where the inexperienced skipper had taken on more than he could manage, what with a new and elaborate sailing cruiser, and a strong wind and awkward sea. His wife, who knew even less about sea-going than he did, took severe fright, so that their daughter too became thoroughly scared, all three of them soon being helplessly seasick.

Their thirteen-year-old son, who had been dragged unwillingly on board without having the slightest interest in any part of the venture, apparently didn't care a hoot if Father wrecked the boat once and for all, so long as *he* could walk off the remains. And incredible as it seems, he simply refused to lift a finger to help! He just sat below, as the mother tearfully told us later, with all hell let loose around him, and read a paperback, not even appearing on deck to aid his exhausted parents in securing the towline from the vessel which had been called out to the rescue by an anxious onlooker standing on what was by then a perilously close and rocky lee shore.

It seems that prior to this awful excursion into the world of boating, the father had done nothing whatever either to try and generate in the rest of his family any kind of interest in the sport, or to learn enough about it himself before committing them to a situation with which he himself could not cope. Fortunately, he sold the boat the very next weekend – a saddened, and probably rather puzzled man.

We freely admit that the two of us have been less than ideal boating parents ourselves; we made plenty of mistakes in the early years. We know, too, of many others who managed the 'middle years', when their youngsters were between say eight and fourteen, far better than we did. However, we think we know where we might have done better, and now that our daughters have grown up, they do still sail with us from time to time!

The parent's holiday – or the child's?

There is an obvious tendency to involve children in the kind of vacation which the parents find most delightful, and compared to many other pastimes, boating, and in particular some form of sailing, is more suited to the tastes of both generations than most. It combines the odd thrill and touch of excitement with a flavour of romance (if you look at it the right way), and a bit of exploration and adventure. It also requires some degree of various skills, so that an annual cruising holiday (or even camping coupled with boating) can be something to which the family can look forward together, and towards which all may join in the planning.

The important thing is for the parents constantly to bear in mind the fact that children see it all rather differently, and are likely to prefer spending more time, say, on beaches, or on the wonder and excitement of night passages (when they will possibly fail to remain awake anyway), than they themselves. For most very young children, the boat is just a means of travelling awfully slowly from one sandy beach or waterside playground, to another.

So if a family is to continue to enjoy boating holidays together, until the time comes for the fledglings to flee the nest, then the way of accomplishing it has to be modified to suit in turn all the individuals concerned. Thus a family skipper may have to forgo making use of a fair wind, in order to please the young in his crew, or explain to them just why anchoring on a lee shore, to let them play in the surf on the beguiling beach they can see, would be too great a risk to the boat. Such decisions can be extremely hard to make – and harder to explain. As in any family situation, there must be some give and take.

The choice of boat best suited to family purposes is discussed in the next chapter. It is worth emphasising that parents and children should be content at least to spend their summer holiday on board, if possible, so as to ensure that the boat pays its way. And that means making sure that right from the start all members of the family really do enjoy and look forward to their holiday afloat.

Families need not of course be confined just to full-blown cruising craft in order to have value for their money; every type of vessel from canoes, racing dinghies, trailable day-sailers to a range of assorted small powered boats can prove every bit as pleasing. A boat doesn't have to be capable even of holding the whole family at one go, so long as everyone gets fun out of her in some way.

Boating is one of the few sports which can be equal fun for all, and happens, into the bargain, to be very good for you. And for your figure, if that is of any concern! The mere fact of being in something which is constantly (however slightly) on the move, whether as a result of the action of waves or just when other people move around in her and so cause her to heel slightly this way or that, exercises one's waistline, back, leg, arm, and neck muscles continually. With ropes to handle, the arm, chest and other muscles of the torso have plenty to do.

Where children are concerned, boating teaches them balance, self-discipline, and above all, the ability to think ahead and act very quickly indeed in a way few other pastimes or mental exercises can equal; and that is something which will stand them in good stead for the rest of their lives.

Even if hiring a boat once in the year is all one can manage, the benefits will be noticeable, so long as the area and type of boat one hires for the family have been chosen with them and their abilities (and limitations) in mind.

With a boat as part of the family, however, the advantage is considerable, for when the craft is there to be worked on, fussed over, taken care of throughout the year, and adventures are there to be dreamed about, a succession of memorable holidays can be planned and experienced in a way which knits the family together in a united action.

Boating grandparents

Well – we expect to be. Many's the cruising boat that will sleep three generations! (From this point of view, most cruising catamarans with their wide cockpit and non-heeling type of sailing have obvious advantages over monohulls of the same length.)

But even if grandparents never come out on the water at all, they will nevertheless want to be kept informed of their family's cruise as it progresses. (A gale warning on the radio concentrates the mind wonderfully!) In the absence of a radio telephone by which to send a stream of reassuring messages, the dutiful skipper or his mate will use the public telephone at convenient ports of call – always assuming that he is cruising in an area where every anchorage possesses such a thing. Areas such as the West Coast of Scotland are not so blessed, and a day or two's delay in finding a convenient phone may well cause unnecessary worry at the other end.

A method of giving the grandparents a share of the action, which we (and they) have found highly satisfactory is to keep a

14

letter to them constantly on the go, like a log-book, posting off instalments every few days. (If the yacht is benefiting from Coastguard surveillance, obtained by applying on a Form CG 66, you will of course be doing a favour to everyone who is concerned for your safety.)

2

Which Kind of Boat?

A chartered boat

Assuming you like the notion of holidays afloat with your family, how do you choose a family boat?

You can put off answering this question, of course, by hiring something suitable for your holiday. A cruise in a hired boat may help you decide your priorities when buying your own.

Many families prefer not to be lumbered with the responsibility and cost of looking after berthing, fitting-out, and maintaining their own boat, especially if they do not live conveniently near to suitable water. For them chartering is always the answer, and the same basic criteria (which we shall discuss) apply when it comes to choosing a suitable craft. One might, however, have to compromise to a greater extent than with one's own boat.

Few hire-boats will have all the 'kiddy refinements' which a family would fit over a period to a privately owned yacht, but some of the various arrangements, such as a jackstay for safety-harnesses, can, if one has the fore-thought to take along a bit of extra line, be arranged without damaging or altering the hired craft in any way.

Those who charter regularly will gradually build up a sort of 'cruising pack' of their own, containing bits of useful gear, like the right size of lifejacket, their oilskins, perhaps their own safety harnesses and one or two favourite navigating instruments, tools, and culinary items, as well as a compact family medicine and First Aid kit, and one or two toys and games.

And if possessed of such a thing, and with the permission of the charter-boat's owners of course, one might also take along one's own extra inflatable or folding (sailing) dinghy, transported on the car roof-rack to the departure point.

Inland waters often provide special interest for children, as compared to the possibility of spending hours at sea with (in their estimation) nothing much to look at, and there are many well-known and highly experienced charter fleets with a wide selection of craft, both on the Norfolk Broads, and the English and Scottish Canal systems, quite apart from what may be available overseas.

The dangers on inland waterways are mainly confined to falling in (more usually from the bank, quayside, or canal lock than from the boat), and from incorrect and careless use of bottled gas. Otherwise, apart from the possibility of the odd bump, this form of boating is about as safe as it could be.

Information on this sort of chartering can be gleaned from *The British Waterways Board, Willow Grange, Church Road, Watford, WD1 3AQ*, and the charter firms who advertise regularly through the yachting press, travel agents, and elsewhere. Both *Hoseasons* and *Blakes* nowadays have excellent fleets of charter boats (mostly power, but some sail) in all sorts of areas as well as the Norfolk Broads. Their addresses are: *Hoseasons Holidays Ltd., Sunway House, Lowestoft, Suffolk, NR32 3LT*, and *Blakes Holidays, Wroxham, Norwich, Norfolk, NR12 8DH*.

Sea-going chartering is a different matter, requiring definite skills, and unless joining a skippered charter boat where the only restriction may be a *minimum* age-limit, the head of the family crew will usually be asked to provide some evidence of his/her sailing experience before being accepted.

Fleet chartering, where a whole fleet of boats cruise in company, thus minimising the amount of experience needed, can be the greatest of fun if you are suitably gregarious, as the children will soon find friends of their own age-group aboard other boats.

Many families like truly to 'get away from it all' and to seek isolation and adventure among (for instance) Scottish lochs or islands, and enjoy being able to make up their own minds, or change them at will, without reference to anyone-else as to where they'll spend the next night. Many charter companies cater for just this sort of holiday. Again, a large number of reputable sea-charter firms advertise regularly in the better sailing magazines, like *Yachting Monthly* and *Practical Boat Owner*, but do be sure and book no later than January or February, if you want to hire during the peak months of July and August. Make certain too just how well the yacht in question will be equipped, especially as regards safety equipment and the more basic things like proper charts of the area you intend to visit, steering and hand bearing-compasses, distance recorder, radio aids, and whatnot. A bit of research well in advance can save an awful lot of disappointments, delays, and spoilt holidays later.

As to the cost of chartering, well it always *seems* terribly pricey, but when you begin to compare it to the annual cost of actual ownership, mooring dues and maintenance, etc., it may not seem excessive. *And at least you would not have to finance a sizeable investment in the first place.* Nor will you suffer those nagging little worries at the back of your mind which most owners sense, when back at home after a cruise and a sudden gale rattles the roof-tiles and thunders in the chimney. Many's the owner who will start up with every squall, and gasp 'I wonder if the boat's all right?'

So, even though a chartered yacht may not be fitted out perfectly to suit the needs of the children, the way a craft of your own would come to be, there's a lot to be said for this more sporadic, once-a-year kind of family boating.

But if you can afford your own personal craft, she can be modified or added to in such a way as to make life safer for small children, and can come to be as much a member of the family in her own right, and as much loved by all, as a dog or cat.

Your own boat

Just how expensive is – for example – a brand-new small cruising boat suitable for maybe a Channel crossing? (Not that that is by any means the smallest or cheapest craft a given family might find adequate for what they want; but a boat of this kind may be considered as 'average'.)

In these days of inflation, there is no sense in quoting actual prices, but if you think in terms of something like twice or three times the price of a *new*, middle-sized saloon car, you won't be too far out. Quite a large capital sum is therefore involved; maybe as much as one might pay for a very small and fairly remote country cottage, though the advantages over a 'holiday home' are enormous, in that a boat is fully mobile and thus offers a wide range of different environments.

Ownership of a boat does mean tying up one's capital, but well-maintained pleasure craft have long been remarkably good investments, even when a marine mortgage or other loan is involved. However that may be, let us consider what a sum of say £8,000 (1982) can do, when it comes to boating versus other kinds of holidays.

If the fellow who scoffs at 'rich men's playthings' has a family of for example wife and two kids, and he takes them all to the Costa Brava each year, he will spend something like £1,000 each time, at 1982 prices. After eight years of this, what has he left? Nothing but a few photographs, mementos, fading memories, and an empty purse.

By contrast, the would-be yachtsman, again with wife and two children, can buy himself a fine, seaworthy little second-hand cruising craft for rather less than £8,000 if he's careful, moor her in a tidal creek or other inexpensive spot, and have year after year of holiday cruising to all sorts of places, for very little more than what he would spend simply staying at home. And at the end of his eight years, when the other chap has nothing left, the boat owner will still have his yacht.

Assuming he has maintained and handled her with reasonable care and caution in the meantime, he could then sell her, even allowing for inflation, for at least as much in real terms as he originally paid. If he does, of course, it will probably be to buy a bigger or better craft to replace her, because he will have discovered that boating offers one of the finest, healthiest, and cheapest kinds of family holiday there is, next to camping under canvas. Not only will he have a sound investment, but his outlay on a family holiday will be far less than if he incurred public transport fares and hotel expenses.

Second-hand sail?

While a good second-hand boat of the kind you might want may seem costly enough compared to one in poor condition, it is still a lot cheaper than a new version of the same thing. The problem is how to tell a good one from a duff one, which maybe has a mass of potentially expensive problems lurking beneath the skin.

The only real answer to this is to go to a firm specialising in marine (preferably yacht) surveying, and spend the necessary fee (usually based on a standard charge formula amounting to something like the length times breadth of the boat in feet, divided by a factor of 2.1, the answer being in Pounds Sterling) for a full, professional survey. It is not cheap, but it may well save you a far greater sum than if you take a chance on something that 'looks alright', and discover later that she wasn't.

Wooden boats can have nice paintwork over rot and a good layer of filler; fibreglass ones can have similarly concealed weakspots where damage, straining, or heavy impacts have been imperfectly repaired or painted over. And the underwater parts should be properly checked for osmosis blistering, or 'boat-pox'.

However, because of the cost and inconvenience of having such a survey carried out (the boat will certainly have to be hauled out, for a start), it will not be worth arranging this unless you are otherwise convinced you have found the vessel you really intend to buy. So check her over as best you can first. In the case of smaller, open boats and dinghies, one can usually detect any disaster areas fairly easily. Don't be rushed. If you don't feel competent to carry out an adequate inspection yourself, find someone (from a boatyard, for example) who is. But beware of a slick paint-job. She may or may not be a perfectly maintained boat with absolutely nothing suspect underneath the gleaming exterior.

What do you want of your boat?

The choice of a boat depends on what you and your family seriously wish to do with it. If it's just whizzing about for fun out on the water, on the odd nice day during a motoring or camping holiday, maybe a small powerboat of some sort may serve you very well indeed.

If on the other hand you are fond of fishing, a small but stable powered craft – again with a second means of propulsion, be it only a stout pair of oars – will probably suit perfectly on inland waters, and for sea-going a larger version, preferably with some kind of shelter and plenty of freeboard (this being the height of the boat's sides above the waterline) when loaded.

Small craft of the above kinds have the added advantage that they do not need a mooring; they can be trailed to and from different places behind any family car with considerable ease (at a maximum speed of 50 mph provided the necessary regulations regarding trailers and reflective triangles and properly lit tail-boards are obeyed).

However, since it may be that neither of the above small powered boat types will hold the enthusiasm of the entire family for very long, something in which you can all sleep, if only for the occasional summer weekend, but preferably for rather longer periods, is likely to prove more interesting. Such a boat with even a tiny cabin of sorts will keep at least some of you dry should the summer weather play tricks now and then.

Especially for the young, the thought of sleeping aboard and doing a bit of 'exploring' in a boat they can 'live' in, holds great appeal – and by 'young' we mean young in spirit, as well as young in age. If there are sails to play with, those who are of sufficient size will have something to do to help make the boat go, other than just sitting about and occasionally being allowed to steer.

And that really brings us to the inescapable fact that the majority of youngsters who go boating will continue to enjoy doing so much longer and with far greater enthusiasm, in our experience, if a sailing boat of some kind is involved right from the start.

Power or sail?

Of course, for many parents the choice of having a sailing or motor boat will depend on their abilities, preferences, and where they like to be afloat (no point in having a deep-keeled gaff cutter if your favourite waters are narrow-boat canals), or of course on what they already own. But for others who are not yet boat-owners but are thinking along those lines, there are two principal considerations. Again, these are their own boating ability, and what use they hope to make of a boat. It's a foregone conclusion that the price may be the guiding factor in either of these.

Taking ability first, parents who know nothing whatever about boating may well feel that they might be safer and more in control of some kind of motorboat, rather than a seemingly unstable and complex-looking sailing craft. Fair enough. Safety is of prime importance, and never more so than when taking youngsters afloat in the early years. It is worth remembering all the same that sailing boats of any size can be used under power, so providing you with two fairly satisfactory means of propulsion. Unless a true powerboat has a 'back-up' auxiliary engine of some sort, or has twin engines with completely separate individual fuel and electrical systems, there is more risk of a fault creating real trouble. A boat is not like a motorcar: one cannot just pull into the side and stop, if one loses motive power at sea. For all that, the relative simplicity of powercraft handling makes such boats widely attractive.

And there lies hidden danger. In Britain, there are no laws to prevent one from buying a 'package deal' in the form of a speedboat with high-powered engine and road trailer from some showroom forecourt, without any form of licence. One is then free to tow it to the nearest lake or seaside bay, and launch and use it without first having learnt a single thing about the Rule of the Road at Sea, not to mention far more basic details concerning the effects of wave-making, tides, currents, winds, or how to handle that particular craft with regard to its manoeuvrability, seaworthiness, or its passing effects on other boats.

Unfortunately, driving a powerboat is in no way similar to

FIG. 1
THE DANGER OF AN OFFSHORE BREEZE

WAVE HEIGHT BARELY SHOWS FROM HERE

driving a car. Even with the simplest outboard-engined dinghy or small launch, there is much that one must learn before setting out, in order to do so safely and without being a nuisance to others. The noise of such craft, never mind the wash they can create at certain speeds, can make you remarkably unpopular!

Off-shore winds are just one of the dangers which are likely to fool the beginner, for though the water may look calm, when you set out, the difference becomes all too apparent when you try to turn back. Where the average speedboat is concerned, however, the biggest of all the risks comes from wave effects. A light-weight craft travelling at speed can all too readily take off on the back of a wave, whether it has been caused by wind or tidal action or by the wake of your own or someone else's boat.

The Royal National Lifeboat Institution magazine repeatedly describes carelessly driven speedboats flipping over, either through having circled over their own wakes, or turned too tightly at speed.

Where any kind of craft, power or sail, is associated with family boating, knowing the Rule of the Road at Sea is only a part of the safety story; careful basic handling knowledge and care is vital.

The snag with speedboats is that while they are in themselves undoubtedly thrilling for the occupants (and especially the driver) for a time, once one has got used to dashing about at high speed, the idea quickly palls, and boredom tends to set in. Only when youngsters are old enough to try water-skiing, the fast powerboat will for a time provide more family fun – until that too becomes boring. (It is quite expensive, as well, not only on fuel, but on equipment such as skis and wet-suits.)

Unfortunately, in harbours, rivers, lakes, or almost any other sheltered piece of water suitable for the fast craft, the effects of their passing are extremely anti-social, and where other boats are moored, there are generally local bye-laws regarding speed limits and the use of water-skis.

Cabin-cruisers

Cabin-cruisers, on the other hand, no matter how small they might be, do have more to offer. Canal cruising in such craft offers much for a family, because though it is (or should be) taken at very low speeds, the proximity of banks and other boats makes it amply exciting; there is much to see at close hand, and fishing and ease of shore-going are obvious attractions for young and old alike.

At sea, such boats have to be handled with great care, a stand-by outboard engine on a bracket over the stern being to our way of thinking as essential then as chart, compass, anchor, full set of lifejackets, and emergency flares.

Internal combustion engines and electrics are notoriously troublesome and unreliable in boats, if only because even the smallest amount of damp, dirt, or deposit in the fuel tank will inevitably get stirred into the system by the motion, and because salt water (and salt air) is so viciously corrosive.

Motor-cruisers and motor-sailers

Going to the bigger motor-cruiser designed for serious sea-going, twin engines, each with its own independent fuel and electrical system, are definitely advisable; either that, or one needs a really reliable stand-by alternative means of propulsion in an otherwise single-engined craft.

Auxiliary sails may be some kind of answer here, but the hull shape must be suitable, or sails will only assist control of the boat in a generally downwind direction – which is so often the last way one wishes to get blown when in trouble afloat, for shelter is more likely to be found to windward.

Some kind of true motor-sailer is therefore an excellent compromise for many families, such boats having good or at least adequate performance whether under power or sail, to take you where you wish to go. The steadying effect of a sail or sails when motoring in open water is also a worthwhile consideration, especially when one has very young children on board. A very great number of boating families, if they can afford to, choose this kind of vessel.

Cruising trailer-sailers and offshore yachts

If one has plans for the family to spend more than just the occasional night or two afloat, something with a fairly sophisticated cabin will be required, and again there are any amount of craft from which to pick one that will fill the bill in other respects too. The pages of current yachting magazines will reveal plenty of enticing advertisements for the wide range of types available, but the things to look for with the safety of small children in mind are associated mainly with the cockpit arrangements and, in the case of cruising boats, the cabin and decks as well. The underwater shape of the boat is important too, for one with bold, 'full' sections will usually keep more upright than one with weaker curves. The same things apply to the full-blown sea-going cruising boat.

Sailing dinghies

Not every type of sailing dinghy is ideal, or even any good at all, for taking the very young or the whole family out in, but the sturdier, less racy kind are generally quite suitable, once you, as skipper or mate, know how to handle such boats safely.

If you do not know how to sail, start by joining a club and getting taught by experts, or else take a proper sailing course with one of the reputable sailing schools such as advertise regularly in the popular sailing journals, *before you attempt to take your family afloat*.

When it comes to deciding on the best size of sailing boat suitable for your particular family, obviously not just the cost, but also the number of individuals involved – and their physical fitness – has to be taken into account.

Speaking in very general terms, 11ft (3.35m) is about the minimum sensible length for say, Mother, Father and one or two children to make a safe outing on sheltered waters. The ubiquitous *Mirror 10* (actually 10ft 10in long, and known more often simply as the *Mirror Dinghy*) is an ideal example. This chubby little plywood boat, of which there are now around sixty-six thousand sailing throughout the world, finds competitive racing fleets of its own class almost anywhere sufficiently wet. It was, however, designed for general use, and can be handled very easily indeed under mainsail only, or with a small outboard-engine, or as a rowing boat. Remarkably stable and roomy for her size, she has full built-in buoyancy as well as a couple of lockers in which to stow the picnic things, etc., and yet is light enough to be carried on the roof-rack of the average saloon car. Two adults can lift a *Mirror Dinghy* without overmuch effort or backstrain.

We mention this boat in some detail simply because she is so universally popular, and because she embodies most of the features that typify the sort of things one should look for in a family dinghy. Many other dinghy classes possess similar attributes, some being in addition built in fibreglass, which requires rather less maintenance than does a wooden boat, so long as one is very careful to avoid grounding them on sharp stones, etc.

And it goes without saying that a family of four, especially where the children are growing rapidly, will prefer something a bit larger when they are all going afloat together.

Nevertheless, many families have been known to squeeze themselves into far smaller boats. When our three kids were *very* tiny, the five of us could sometimes be seen sailing into little creeks and rivers, or around sheltered anchorages, in our 8ft 6in (2.6m) semi-folding *Puffin* yacht tender. Laden thus, the little boat didn't exactly sparkle to windward, but she gave us endless fun when conditions were right. The *Puffin* it was who taught our children how to sail single-handed, for her beamy little hull, modest rig and utter simplicity, coupled again with built-in buoyancy, made her safe and easy to learn in.

The larger kind of pure racing dinghy will be fine once the children are fully grown and wanting plenty of highly energetic thrills and spills – but such craft are not for beginners or for the very tiny.

One great advantage of a boat small and light enough to be carried on the car-top, is that she can be so easily taken to and (with suitable permission, if required) launched into almost any wayside stretch of water for an afternoon's sail. The same applies to larger trailable dinghies, and to some extent to what have become known as 'trailer/sailers' too, but there is then the problem of leaving a car unattended in a public place with an empty trailer (hopefully locked on) advertising to any potential thief that you aren't likely to be back for an hour or two. A car with a roof-rack, on the other hand, is perhaps less of a 'give-away'.

The heavier the boat, the greater the difficulty and expense involved in launching and recovery. 'The smaller the boat,' some say, 'the greater the fun.'

Certainly, something like a dinghy which can be raced with a local class is going to appeal very much to your children, so long as you can teach them to handle her themselves, once they have grown to a suitable weight and strength.

The trouble is that parental instinct makes one naturally rather averse to risking very tiny children in a boat which might easily be capsized, with or without an expert father or mother at the helm, so many parents prefer to take their little ones sailing in something less likely to tip everyone out.

Launching and retrieving larger craft

The problems increase in proportion to the size and weight of a boat. Even with a very efficient, well-designed trailer, equipped with winch, keel-rollers and all the rest of it, launching and recovery onto the trailer after one's sail can be a bit tricky. Launching is only likely to be really bothersome in a strong wind, or if the bottom happens to be rather too soft, so that the wheels of the trailer sink in. One then has to push the boat clear physically or wait for the tide to lift her off, which is the more sensible thing to do if one has the patience, if there *is* a tide, and if it isn't ebbing!

Recovery, on the other hand, can often be a bit fraught. Locating the boat accurately over the trailer is the main difficulty, and there is often a tendency to use muscle power to help the process. This may be fine and well for fit young Rugby players with a penchant for weight-lifting in the evenings, but for those whose job or normal physical activity is seldom more strenuous than climbing the office stairs when the lift has given up, it can be surprisingly dangerous.

Beware of back injuries

The act of trying to lift and haul a stuck boat often necessitates simultaneous twisting and lifting, which combined with a pull is the quickest way we know to strain unaccustomed muscles, or to 'put a disc out'. Disc lesions are in fact an extremely common injury amongst those who indulge only sporadically in this type of boating. But because the boat *looks* as though you could, with a bit of a heave, lift and tug her into place, one naturally tends to try.

The answer is to work every move out beforehand, whenever possible; not just the order of doing things, but who, of the family strong enough to be useful even if only for the lighter jobs, should be positioned where, to do what.

A lot will depend on the type of trailer used, and on the shape of your boat's underwater parts. The possible variations are too numerous to list here, but in our experience a couple of garden bamboo canes, if stronger 'docking guides' cannot be used, fixed upright at the sides of the trailer to act as guides when you are aligning the boat over it, will generally prove invaluable. In any event, a full understanding by all concerned of what will (or should) happen, and in which sequence, will help to make the whole job simple, straightforward and easy.

One word of warning: do keep children (and unthinking adults) away from the 'downhill' end of the trailer whether the latter is stopped or moving; if it breaks loose and someone is in the way, the result can be appalling. Keep them away from near the wheels also, and clear of any ropes if they are not actively engaged in helping in a competent manner.

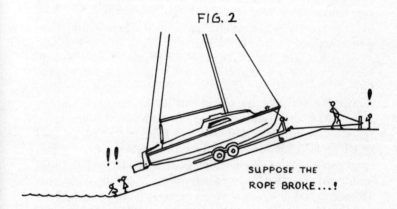

FIG. 2

SUPPOSE THE
ROPE BROKE...!

Day-sailer open boats

Most firms producing the sort of open day-sailers which are particularly popular these days, have given pretty careful thought to the trailer system recommended for each type of boat. Often one can buy the boat, all her gear, the trailer, outboard engine and everything else, as a package, so that the business of launching and recovery has already been worked out and matched to the craft. If not, take the advice of the builders, or of any other owners of that sort of boat you can find.

One might well wish to know *which* of the abundant boats

available in this classification is the one for your particular family, and luckily there is a fairly easy way to find out. Go and look, preferably, at one of the major boat shows, such as Earls Court, or Southampton, and see what takes your fancy within your price bracket – and then *arrange for a demonstration sail*. If at all possible, you should try and get a demonstration of how to launch and recover the boat in question as well. That way you can assess whether or not you think you and your family could cope.

Where you will be sailing with the very young on board, something really stable (non-heeling to any great extent), with full, built-in buoyancy, good freeboard, and a simple, not too lofty rig will be best. This, however, usually means pretty heavy construction, so whatever the length of the boat, a winch mounted on the trailer will be a great help. There is little joy in lying propped up in a chair staring wistfully at your beautiful new craft glistening in the sunshine of your garden, simply because you have wrecked your back the first time you had her out!

There are many such open boats on the market nowadays; some, like the *Drascombe Lugger*, with quite remarkable reputations for seaworthiness. And fame of that sort is well worth looking for. So successful was this original 18ft 9in (5.7m) design with its simulated clinker GRP hull, yawl rig, and boomless sails, that two smaller models of equally traditional appearance, and a pair of larger versions (with small cabin or cuddy forward) have since been produced by Honnor Marine of Totnes, Devon in addition. It is worth noting that the whole concept of the *Drascombe* range was based on 'the requirements of the average family'.

Where to launch

The great benefit on the trailer-sailer type of boat, be she small or as much as maybe 22ft (6.7m) long, is that the choice of sailing water can then be as varied as the amount of fuel you are prepared to put into the towing vehicle.

Most people find it worth while belonging to a yacht club or sailing club on whose waters they will do most of their weekend boating. Belonging to a 'recognised' club has a further advantage; it can mean that when you visit the waters of some other yacht club, you are likely to be well received and perhaps offered the hospitality and facilities thereof, during your stay. Even if you are not a very 'clubby' sort of family, you may at least enjoy being able to leave your road-trailer and possibly your car on the property of such clubs, with the permission of the Secretary and Flag Officers.

Perhaps the best information is to be found in a booklet called *Where to Launch Your Boat* produced annually by Link House Publications, Dingwall Avenue, Croydon, Surrey, CR9 2TA. In some areas, Tourist Information Bureaux can also be a source of directions as to the whereabouts of Public Slipways.

The Royal Yachting Association is the best place to get a list of the addresses of practically all Britain's recognised yacht, sailing and boat clubs, and since this body constitutes a sort of Yachtsman's Union capable of swinging quite heavy metal when it comes to clashes with Authority in whatever form, joining it to start with is not a bad idea. The address is: The Royal Yachting Association, Victoria Way, Woking, Surrey.

Having found out where the various clubs are, one has only to write to a likely one in the area of your choice (in plenty of time before your planned visit) and ask if there might be launching facilities available for the sort of boat you own. Mention the club you belong to, and ask what restrictions apply in the waters you wish to use. Check too whether you will require some kind of permit, as for instance on all British canals, and many meres, lakes, reservoirs and other inland waters.

Nowadays, alas, there are all too few places where you can just turn up, launch, and go off enjoying yourselves for free.

How free is the sea, then?

Very – once you're out on it. To get there from most places it may however be necessary to launch in and pass through somebody's harbour – and for that there will almost certainly be a small fee in the form of harbour dues.

We always feel that having to pay dues is fair enough unless they seem truly exorbitant, in which case we still pay, but simply avoid returning to that particular port again, if we can. Unless you pay dues, how can you expect piers, steps, quayside water supplies, and occasional dredging to be seen to properly on your and everyone else's behalf? So some kind of charge is usually justifiable.

We also have found Harbour Masters on the whole very helpful and friendly – so long as we didn't go bothering them at awkward moments or when there was obviously a rush on, and so long as we always made it clear we were in no great hurry and would gladly fit in with whatever arrangement was most convenient. Most Harbour Masters have a knowledge of the locality which can be most useful if it is proffered, so whether we actually needed advice on the local waters or not, we sometimes found it worth seeking his thoughts on the matter, so long as he seemed to have time to talk. If he had, an invitation on board the yacht never went amiss, either, and frequently resulted in a valuable and subsequently most welcoming friendship.

The trouble with the 'free' part of the sea is that it is not always a suitable place on which to venture in a small boat, particularly if she's open and rather heavily laden with kids, etc. The enclosed waters of harbours, apart from being anyway quite interesting, will be much more sheltered and calm, as will any slow-moving narrow waterway, and most inland lakes.

Areas such as Chichester Harbour, the Beaulieu River, Christchurch and Poole Harbours on the South Coast of England, which abound in fascinating creeks, offer much for the family man with a small open boat. And many of the rivers of the Thames Estuary, in Kent, Essex, and Suffolk will allow for days, weeks, and even years of exploration for the trailer-sailer.

The Norfolk Broads are another matter, more given over to hire-craft users.

Further north on the East Coast of England, and even up on the Eastern Coast of Scotland, conditions are rugged with little shelter if it comes on to blow.

There are one or two excellent areas in Devon and Cornwall, as well as in the South-western corner of Wales, where rivers wind seawards among steep, tree-lined banks and small craft find a sort of heaven. Many people, on the other hand, feel it very worth while to brave the occasional raindrop and not nearly so occasional midge (or so it can seem at times), plus maybe a long haul by road, to cruise among the myriad isles and sea-lochs which together offer many hundred miles of truly superb sailing in the magnificent scenery of the West Coast of Scotland.

In May or June particularly the weather there, though chilly at night sometimes, is at its best. In July and August, the school holiday times, it is warmer but less reliable, some years. The other rewards, however, make up for any meteorological short-comings; in strong winds one can still find sheltered waters, and in light airs one's boat will glide across unbroken reflections of mountain and glen, or come to her anchor at the head of a narrow, heather-clad sea-loch, or tucked behind some low, rocky islet. One can often sail downwind there, rather than having to beat, for anchorages are plentiful and seldom more than one hour's sail apart, with a choice in several directions. And as often as not the wind direction will be different the next day.

On the Scottish West Coast, and in Hebridean waters in general, harbour dues are rarely charged, unless you lie alongside in a recognised port. Lying to your own anchor is normally free, and in any case most of the best-sheltered anchorages are completely natural and frequently devoid of houses, roads, or people, let alone any kind of harbour works. Neither are there any refuse collections in such out-of-the-way havens – see pp. 121–5.

Apart from the possible complication and expense of trailing your boat there by often hilly roads, Scotland's West Coast waters are probably the cheapest and yet most unspoilt and beautiful cruising ground in Britain.

In Ireland, although there are few good yacht harbours on the East Coast, other than Howth, the North of Ireland possesses one absolute *dream* of an area for family boating, in the shape of Strangford Lough in County Down. Here, among the low, humpy green islands and winding sounds, we did much of our earliest sailing when our children were little. Still tidal waters, the strange creatures of the shallows, peaceful nights at anchor, and the call of wild birds are marvellous surroundings to show any child.

The Western side of Ireland, like that of Scotland, is ragged with inlets, some large and impressive and others small and fascinating. However, without the sheltering string of the Outer Hebrides to hide behind, its seaward coastline is wide open to the full width of the Atlantic, and the swell that batters its grey-rock cliffs makes it a place for none but the true seaman and best of seaboats.

Inland in the North of Ireland, the best freshwater cruising and boating area is unquestionably among the tortuous banks of Upper Lough Erne, where a number of well-run charter firms take advantage of the safe water and beautiful surroundings.

The Republic in the South, Eire, has something even better, if the criterion is the distance one can sail (or rather motor). Many, many people have sung the praises of the wonderful Shannon Waterway.

The area you choose will depend on time available, travelling distances, what takes your fancy, and more important surely than anything else, the sort of boat you have. The day will come, if you begin by playing things gently, when your young will easily out-do you in ambitions.

The child-proof yacht

There are obviously many things about a boat which could be a source of injury or danger to very small children, apart from the risk of their falling overboard, being hit by ropes or spars, or having fingers or toes caught or broken.

Such hazards will be discussed at some length later, so for the moment let us look at the basic design features which an ideal family boat might have.

The first problem many people are likely to come across when going afloat with a carrycot or other suitably wrapped infant will be in transferring the baby from shore to ship. Guardrails (lifelines) rather hinder the procedure, but are so essential otherwise that the answer will probably be to fit them with some kind of gate at a suitable point, opened by means of slip-clips. With some plastic-coated wire lifelines, the wire forward and aft of the gate may go slack when the latter is opened, and anyone then moving on the sidedeck, perhaps to let other people pass, might lean on some part which won't support them as expected, with dampening results.

For this and other reasons, we have always employed pre-stretched Terylene rope rather than wires, so that suitable stopper-knots can be tied either side of the gate stanchions to prevent slippage. The rest of the rail thus remains taut whether the gate is open or closed. Another good point in favour of rope lines, as opposed to plastic-coated wire ones, is that you can *see* when they are chafed or likely to break.

A large but well-protected cockpit is best. Deep, sheltering coamings are especially useful, not just to keep youngsters from being thrown out if the ship lurches, but to keep wind and spray off them. At sea, children will often become still for long periods, reading, drawing, or just dreaming. Queasiness can have the same effect with some, while others find the motion lulling and sleepy-making. Immobility, from whatever cause, can result in a small body becoming chilled right through very quickly, so shelter from the wind is extremely important.

Where a cockpit is high up, maybe with seats at the same level as the deck, anyone can see that the risks, both of exposure and of falling out are greater than where the boat has a deeper, more sheltered one, but it is possible to improve things even with a shallow one by rigging a set of spray dodgers in the lifelines. Better still, in our opinion, is a hood or canopy over the fore part of any family cruising boat's cockpit and cabin hatchway. If it incorporates some form of window through which the helmsman can see without undue vision distortion, it is likely to remain up and in use both in port and at sea all the time, and becomes a very popular part of the ship.

Children who tend anyway to be travel-sick, not usually as infants but later on (see p. 54 & pp. 98–102), need plenty of fresh air, so such good positive shelter at the forward end of the

35

cockpit, out of the way of ropes and those working the ship, is most valuable.

Further forward in any boat the motion is worse, and while a cabin affords protection from the cold and spray, it can sometimes be dark, noisy, and frightening down there when conditions outside are a bit boisterous. If there is no proper shelter on deck in these circumstances, the next best thing will be a well-ventilated cabin which has seating at a height from which children can readily see out.

How about two hulls?

From this and other points of view, a catamaran may well be worth considering when the children are young. In most of these boats, the saloon is usually on the bridge-deck, and its side windows are often at exactly the right height for children sitting there to see through without having to stand up or crane their necks. (This does not of course apply in the true Double-Canoe Wharram-type catamaran, which has all its accommodation down in the hulls, without any shelter on the bridgedeck between them.)

Catamarans have the added advantage where the very young are concerned (not to mention their parents and grandparents too), of rarely heeling more than about 8 degrees to the water surface. This renders passage-making infinitely less tiring physically (for everyone), and means that except in very rough conditions, toys, cooking implements and gear stay more or less where they have been put down, instead of rolling or falling 'downhill' each time the boat changes tack. One also spends much less time in stowing for sea in such craft.

After many happy years of sailing all sorts of monohulled boats, we ourselves decided after an impressive trial weekend, to do the sort of cruising we thought would be suitable for our small daughters to enjoy, in a catamaran. We never once regretted the choice.

Due however to the conservative nature of most sailing people, plus the fact that certain early and rather too sporty makes of cruising cats had gained notoriety through occasionally capsizing, one may feel an instinctive reluctance to consider this sort of boat – especially where one's offspring are to be involved. Since those early days, however, much has been learned about multihull design, and there are a number of excellent, and superbly seaworthy cruising cats available nowadays of which none has capsized, for all that many hundreds of those particular designs have been sailed for thousands of miles in various parts of the world.

The merits and disadvantages (for there are some) of this type of vessel are discussed in full in *Catamarans for Cruising* by Jim Andrews (also published by Hollis & Carter).

Catamarans nevertheless do not seem ideal to everyone; higher harbour dues are sometimes charged (seldom justifiably) than for monohulls of similar beam and greater lengths, and catamarans are a bit less general in scope, especially where it comes to racing. It is likely that some sailing fathers may not feel that their personal sailing dreams and yearnings are fully satisfied unless they can indulge in one or two passage-races during the year, and it should be pointed out that while we personally have considered catamarans exceptionally suitable for family *cruising*, we have never held the view that such craft are entirely ideal for racing. (It goes without saying that we know several cat designers who will disagree, but this is *our* opinion, not theirs.) The main reason behind this, to our way of thinking, is that whereas a ballasted monohull of good design can sometimes be pushed with impunity right up to her limits, doing the same in a catamaran imposes colossal strains on the rig, so that if anything does go wrong it will probably do so drastically. This includes capsizing.

One has always to weigh the admittedly horrifying possibility of certain types of cruising cat inverting, against that of almost *any* ballasted monohull being holed by floating debris (or otherwise filling with water) and rapidly sinking. All one can add to such an appalling picture is that most modern catamarans will continue to float whether holed or capsized, and in either case are likely to remain very visible, especially from the air, owing to their comparatively large, oblong deck (or bottom) area. And as has several times been demonstrated in one or two of the really very few inversions that have occurred, the crew is normally able to get out of (or if need be, back into) the cabin without overmuch difficulty, and are, if nothing else, left at least with something solid and fairly obviously 'not right', on which to await rescue.

It's a thoroughly unbearable subject to contemplate when talking of sailing with one's family, but for all that we considered the capsize risk minimal even in the least stable of the three cruising catamarans we enjoyed, in the first place because we were careful about the choice of design, and secondly because we attempted always to handle our boats with a degree of caution and common seamanship.

So despite the fact that our favourite cruising-ground (the West Coast of Scotland) is known for its frequently strong winds and exceedingly heavy and sudden squalls, in over sixteen years and something like eleven thousand nautical miles of catamaran cruising in all kinds of weather, we never once came near to flying a hull, let alone capsizing. (This wasn't just in sheltered waters; the Minches are not that, any more than are the English Channel and full length of the Irish Sea, which we navigated more than once.) Hebridean meteorology has caught us out with unforecast Force 7 and 8 on too many occasions to recall, even though we always tried to avoid such conditions; but even then, or when trapped in some remote anchorage in the flying spray of a shrieking Force 10, we never once felt that any of our catamarans gave us cause for fear.

As with other kinds of boat, it is a matter of choosing the right sort of design for the job you wish to carry out, and then conducting the vessel in question reasonably within her own capabilities, and yours. As always where boats are concerned, the choice of craft and one's usage of her must boil down simply to common sense and seamanship.

So in answer to those who in the past let it be known to us that they considered it rash of us (to put it mildly) to take young children to sea in an *unballasted* sailing boat, our answer was always this: 'Do you really think we *would* take them, if there *was* the slightest risk over and above those normally experienced afloat?'

We, after all, were and are as doting as most normal parents tend to be, and on reflection now believe there may have been numerous times when we were a bit too protective and cautious.

Three hulls suit some . . .

As to trimarans, there seem to be very few really good ones that are genuinely suitable for family cruising. They sail at greater angles of heel than catamarans in anything of a breeze, and length for length have less accommodation than a monohull usually, whereas a catamaran has a lot more. But it's all a matter of what you like.

Trimarans generally handle more like monohulls, and will often turn out average speeds of something like a knot faster, taken over an entire cruise. Catamarans on the other hand require slightly different handling in some circumstances, and though not perhaps quite so dashing as some trimarans, still tend to average noticeably more over a season's cruising than monohulls of a similar length.

A stiff boat means a relaxed family

The important thing about any kind of yacht which is to be used primarily for family sailing when children are small, is that she should not heel too readily or too much. She must also be capable of being managed entirely by one person without help, at least while on passage.

A boat which sails at great angles of heel presents all sorts of difficulties when it comes to the secure stowing of small items, and makes the playing of board and other games almost impossible when under way in fresh winds. Children aged less than about eight or ten seldom take much interest in the boat's progress, or in passing coastal scenery such as may delight their parents, so plenty of other ways of occupying them between harbours has to be found. It naturally helps if they can safely spread toys and books around without the boat tipping the whole lot onto the floor every time she encounters a squal'.

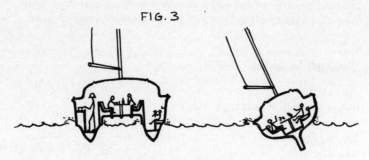

FIG. 3

STABILITY & UPRIGHTNESS
MAKE FOR RELAXATION

Worse, however, are the effects of such a craft on the cooking of food. (Never mind the eating of it!) Hot food, drinks, and plenty of snacks are the best defence for adults, and even more so for children, against seasickness and fatigue, not to mention the insidious onset of thorough chill. If the boat is perpetually canted over on her ear, even the simplest galley task, be it merely pouring out a few mugfuls of soup from a vacuum flask, becomes arduous and fraught. When the yacht is leaping up and down and possibly lurching sideways now and then as well, providing the crew with hot sustenance can become almost impossible.

So if you possibly can, choose a yacht which you have reason to believe can carry her canvas without heeling too much. And if you can find a design which isn't greatly given to pitching and plunging as well, your family may well find themselves enjoying the occasional really rough sail, simply because they need spend less time and effort in clinging on and/or feeling unwell.

Single-handed – with the family on board

Our comment about easy handling is born the hard way, of our own experiences when sailing with very young infants. Human nature being what it is, Mother is usually more concerned about keeping her little ones amused or fed or emptied as the case may be, than she is about doing the things that Father manages better, at least where muscle counts. And since, when the kids are on board, the handling of sheets and changing sails or reefing is then normally carried out by him, while Mother briefly takes the helm, he is likely to find himself left completely solo on watch between-times, possibly for hours on end. It might happen, when we were entering some strange harbour, in the dark, with both of us alert and at the ready on deck: there we would be, all keyed up for whatever action might suddenly be required, when a piercing shriek from below, or despairing cry of '*Potteee!*' would have Mate-cum-Mother disappear, leaving Father desperate for another pair of hands! Of course, if such action would *really* have endangered the vessel, our ears would have been shut, heedless of the consequences in the cabin, and the requisite tasks on deck would have been completed with stoicism until the ship was safe. But maternal instinct is a remarkably powerful force!

We very soon learned to turn *Twintail*, our original 27ft cruising catamaran, into a most passable single-hander, so that either of us could handle her in practically all likely situations, without assistance from the other.

A boat whose cockpit, engine controls and sail plan are laid out in such a way as to make single-handing possible, is therefore, to our way of thinking, vital when small children are on board, unless you happen to have a third adult crew-member to help.

Things like an efficient roller headsail system, and some kind of automatic steering, whether electronic or wind-powered, will prove a boon to the skipper of a young sailing family.

Deck safety

Another important factor is the security of those on deck. Being virtually single-handed, while one's spouse is below caring for your offspring, is one thing – she will probably have time (and should be able) to navigate for you, and to pass out course alterations, snacks, and other encouragements during a long spell at the helm. However, if in the course of performing some action on deck you get pitched over the lee rail, the urgent question arises as to whether the person left will be able to cope not only with the extremely difficult task of handling the yacht, finding you, and getting you back on board, but of managing to do so with a gaggle of possibly quite distressed children milling around underfoot at the same time.

The answer to this question is rather unlikely to be 'yes'.

Rigid adherence to certain safety disciplines, whether for Skipper, Mate, or child, is therefore imperative. A jackstay, or track and slides, for safety-harness clips, rigged along the length of the ship, are very much better than the normal business of having to clip on, unclip, and clip on again in a series of precarious progressions, in order to reach the foredeck from the cockpit.

Chapter 4 deals in detail with suitable safety equipment, lifejackets, and all the rest of it. What we are concerned with at the moment, are actual features of the boat's basic design and layout.

Clear the decks!

A further important safety aspect both for children and adults, is the width of a boat's sidedecks, if any. The wider the better. So often one comes across small craft where the sidedeck is barely broad enough for a sailing-shoe, and with boots and oilskins restricting movements, a cabintop on one side and guardrail stanchions on the other, progress can then be really tricky when the ship is heeled and the decks slippery. In some boats things are made even worse by the shroud rigging, round or under which one has to squeeze with attendant risks to equilibrium, so these features should be carefully assessed before deciding on a particular design, if one is buying afresh or chartering, come to that.

On the deck itself, toe-catching fittings should be avoided, not just physically but altogether, if they can be. Whatever mooring cleats or sheet fairleads there are on the sidedecks should ideally be as near the rail or as out of the foot-way as possible. Quite apart from the dangers of tripping during a sudden dash forward, there are the agonising toe or ankle injuries which can all too easily occur: deck shoes have their virtues, even on summer days.

Anything which can put *any* member of the family crew out of action, however temporarily, can lead to a chain of further troubles if circumstances turn the wrong way.

'Can I steer, daddy?'

There are times even in quite large yachts when three-year-olds may safely be allowed to steer for a while. Wheel steering is usually regarded by Junior as being much more fun – and sometimes more comprehensible – than tiller steering, in that it avoids the concept imposed by a tiller of having to 'push the stern round' in order to point the boat in the desired direction. Through gearing, a wheel is often easier for young arms to operate, and there is not the same risk of a kick from the rudder causing an injury. On the other hand, wheels can trap unwary little hands, so it's a matter of opinion where the greater danger lies. One might also argue that in general wheels tend to be less 'direct' than tillers, and the 'feel' that a tiller transmits will give the young helmsman an extra sense of being completely 'in charge'. There are points on both sides.

We believe it boils down to the size of the vessel in question, and the amount of helm that she tends to carry in the normal way. If she is going to tug a bit in anything of a breeze, or if the rudder is large, a wheel may well be the more useful answer from a child's viewpoint.

But how does one know in advance what way this or that boat will behave? It's difficult, but one might try listening carefully to others who have experience of her particular type. The other thing is to read whatever 'boat-test' reports have been published on the design in the yachting press, if you really have no possible way of trying her out yourself, before buying.

We would never advise anyone to *buy* any boat, no matter how reputable, until they had first spent at least two hours under way in her, trying her thoroughly for themselves.

There is a further point to look for, on the steering side. Teaching children to steer competently is valuable, as well as fun, and a lot of satisfaction can be derived by both parties. But the youngster must be able to see ahead properly *and comfortably*, from the steering position (see p. 135). So when sizing up the possibilities, bear short backs and little legs in mind. If there isn't a suitable perch built in to the boat you have (or are thinking of buying or chartering) try to envisage some method of rigging a secure 'high chair' or perhaps a folding footstool, to make these occasions – however brief they may at first tend to be – more easy and relaxed for the young navigator.

Rigs

Helping to manage the ship is the best of fun, and welds a family into a feeling of being part of the whole business of boating. Whether the yacht is a sailing dinghy, pocket cruiser, one-time ocean-racer, or a motorboat with some kind of steadying canvas, being allowed to hoist and trim a sail when conditions permit can be most rewarding to the young person, as it makes them genuinely feel a true part of the crew.

A boat which has at least one small, easily handled sail is clearly going to be preferable in the family context to one with no sail at all, or with just a couple of really large ones. Ketches and yawls have the advantage of a mizzen, which is usually small enough for youngsters to control, whenever course alterations or the trimming of sheets is required. A cutter, with her two headsails, also offers more possibilities for children than would the one large foresail of a sloop, in that the inner staysail will often be easily managed by those without much pull.

Chinese lugsails and American-style 'catboat' rigs

The modern version of the traditional fully battened Chinese lugsail, though often quite sizeable in area, is semi-balanced (part of it being forward of the mast to equalise pressure), and thus puts very little load on the sheets, as a rule. From this point

44

of view, it might well be worth considering, where help from the younger members of your crew is concerned, as well as from the viewpoint of reefing, hoisting, or stowing from the cockpit.

Since the advent of sailing surf-boards and the simple, unstayed rig which came with them, several full-sized cruising yachts have been developed with similar but of course much larger unsupported pole masts, sleeved sails, and wishbone booms. Setting no headsails as such, this rig is also extremely easily handled. Sometimes the sail is hoisted conventionally, using slides in a mast-track as on the more traditional modern mainsails, but either way, the simplicity and efficiency of these latest cat-rigged ketches (they usually sport two masts), is impressive. In our opinion, such a rig is also worthy of particular consideration by the would-be cruising parents of young children. The little *Liberty 22* designed by David Thomas is a good example from this point of view and from the fact that she can be trailed behind a middle-sized family car.

To be fully enjoyed and loved by a family, a boat must of course please the eye and the heart simultaneously, and be practical for the use expected of her into the bargain. And as any married person knows, there's no real way of explaining those criteria! Seamen used to say: 'What looks right, is right' – and there's something in that.

Up anchor!

Foredeck work is another field in which children often like to help, though there are obvious dangers where the handling of warps and especially chain are involved, not to mention getting fingers trapped by the moving parts of an anchor.

However, one of the blessings of youth, especially around the age of ten, is a delight in being able to show off growing strength. Thus, if a boat of 24ft (7.2m) or more, overall, can be fitted with a manually operated anchor-winch, this excess energy can be put to raising the hook from time to time, to the mutual satisfaction of both skipper and crew. (Even the job of working a power-winch can be given to an alert child, though this of course does nothing to burn muscle-power.)

The tender behind (on tow)

A most important consideration in any cruising boat is the yacht tender, but dinghies come in so many different guises that one can scarcely begin to commend any particular type. Once the children are old enough to row off on their own, two dinghies are almost essential (see pp. 148–9). A cheap plastic inflatable will suffice perfectly well for the second dinghy. We used one for years, with increasing patches. Such a craft is ideal for a rowing tutor, in that anyone who can row one of those things in a straight line, can thereafter manage pretty well anything with oars!

If one of the dinghies can be made to sail, the enjoyment, and general skill in helming, will be increased a thousand-fold. Small sailing tenders are on the increase, as more families come to realise the benefits (quieter anchorages with fewer outboards, and a cheap means of getting ashore without the effort of rowing, for a start).

Several kinds of inflatable can nowadays be bought with sailing gear, and there are a number of suitable small 'solid' yacht-tenders, too, which sail extremely well. We found the 8ft 6in (2.6m) *Puffin* (as mentioned on p. 27), which has a solid bottom part with built-in buoyancy and fold-down fabric topside extensions ideal for our particular use, and often carried her inverted and 'collapsed' on *Twintail's* cabintop.

There are now other kinds of wooden sailing dinghies which fold even flatter, and yet are rigid enough to be load-bearing and to row well. A visit to Earls Court or Southampton Boat Shows, and an eye kept on yachting press advertisements, will give an idea of the various possibilities.

3

Infants Afloat

Contrary to all our expectations, we found that taking babies sailing in their carrycots was not at all difficult, and in fact a good deal easier than it was when they were a year or two older. Very tiny babies lie content so long as they are being subjected to movement; you don't have to stop them crawling overboard or into the engine-space. And when you put them down, that's where they stay, so long as they are securely wedged in.

The biggest problems come not so much with the baby as with all the gear which accompanies them, starting with the carrycot itself.

Getting them on board

If you can use the sort of carrycot which has a plastic rather than fabric outer skin, salt-spray is kept at bay and will not leave a ring of difficult-to-remove white crystals when it dries. Plastic carrycots are also likely to float, at least for a time, in a sudden emergency. You may well say 'Perish the thought', but it's a consideration. A cover and hood of the same material will also be of use, especially when cot and contents are brought out for an airing on the lee side of the cockpit, where down-draughts off the sails may otherwise be a bother.

Very tiny infants will, in our opinion, be less prone to injury if loaded into the dinghy or passed from shore to ship in the carrycot, rather than 'loose', or in some kind of papoose. The cot offers good protection from the almost inevitable knocks or jerks, and can be handed aboard quite easily.

A papoose – one of those fabric affairs in which the baby can be carried either on its parent's back or chest – is possibly better in that it leaves both the parent's hands free, but if of the kind where the infant is carried at your back, there is the risk of a knock from something you have not seen (because it's behind you). The sort where the baby is held against your chest is preferable in this respect, but makes clambering aboard a yacht from the dinghy extremely difficult, and is harder on the back muscles when going for walks.

FIG. 4

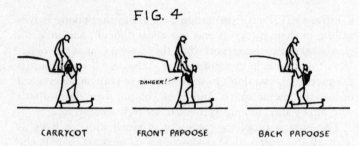

CARRYCOT   FRONT PAPOOSE   BACK PAPOOSE

Otherwise, for shore-going expeditions where rough ground is to be covered, the papoose-type is ideal. Again, it's a matter of choice as to whether you go for the knapsack-like 'back-pack' or the sort you wear in front. With the latter you can keep an eye on the contents – though it's not usually the part you can see that's the worrying bit . . . Carrycots, even when slung between two adults, are less adaptable, unless a set of wheels and passable pavements are available. But they are ideal on board.

A further feature to look for when choosing a boating carrycot is the type of strut involved – assuming that the cot is designed to fold more or less flat, as many are. If you can get the sort with 'bent rod' struts, where the section of the rod is round rather than made out of strips of sheet-metal, you will find that varnished wood on or against which the cot might be placed, will suffer less from the constant jiggling which most carrycot incumbents seem to generate.

Few loaded carrycots are really light, so if it can be placed low down in the dinghy on the way out to your ship, and still keep dry, so much the better; it goes without saying that it should *never* be perched on top of other gear, sail-bags, or whatever, where the wash of a careless passing powercraft might send it slithering, contents and all ... We always had somebody either keep an arm over the cot if it had to be at seat level, or hold onto it one way or another. We did not think it a good idea to tie it to the dinghy, just in case of a capsize.

Bow and stern painters

Obviously a really sturdy, stable dinghy is of prime importance; in other words, one with plenty of beam for its length. Inflatables are excellent in this respect, though any sharp projections on things like carrycots could be a hazard. And because most inflatables have flat bottoms, it is hard to keep water away from anything put thereon.

'Solid' dinghies, of wood or plastics, are better in the latter respect, but rarely have quite the same initial stability, unless of the 'cathedral' hull, or semi-catamaran configuration.

Whatever design or build of dinghy, we found the most difficult thing was constantly to remember to avoid taking those little chances with it which, as competent swimmers, we had been accustomed to risking for convenience, before the baby came along.

Having arrived safely alongside in the dinghy, a great deal will now depend on what type of yacht you are dealing with – how high the topsides are, how the lifelines (guardrails) are rigged, whether there is a boarding ladder or not, and whether you board alongside abreast of the cockpit, or right aft across the stern at the transom. Whichever it is, the very first thing to do is to *secure the dinghy at both ends*, bow *and* stern.

Surprisingly few modern dinghies are even fitted with a point of attachment for a stern painter; usually there is provision only for a single bow rope. So *before* you take Junior out, rig up a proper stern rope on the dinghy.

In order to make the securing of the dinghy quick and easy (so as to leave little excuse for laziness), we used a good length of bow painter, and a short stern rope, and each had a loop at the free end, which could simply be dropped over the appropriate deck cleat at the stern; the stern rope led there direct, and the bow painter was first led forward and round one of the guardrail stanchions, then taken aft. This way there was no chance of either undoing itself just as the precious bundle was being passed to those on board, allowing the dinghy to slide out, out, and away . . . That of course is the danger – that the very act of transferring weight (carrycot) from dinghy to ship, automatically thrusts the dinghy in the opposite direction. Unless the little boat is tightly secured at each end, a widening watery gap suddenly develops at the crucial moment.

Bow and stern painters are therefore an absolute Must, and if really quick and easy to secure, have more chance of being used – every time.

FIG. 5

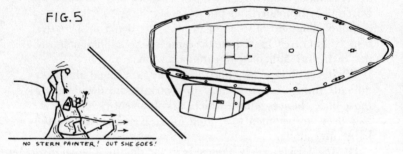

NO STERN PAINTER! OUT SHE GOES!

IMPORTANCE OF BOW AND STERN PAINTERS

In the case of our first boat, a conventional ketch, and later also with our first catamaran, we always boarded alongside rather than over the stern. As the dinghy ranged alongside, whoever was nearest the bow would pass the bow painter round the midships stanchion base, and hand the looped end back to the person in the stern. That person, as the boat dropped back, would then simply hitch the loops of both painters over the cleat on the quarter, and that would be that.

Boarding at the stern, the normal procedure in many modern yachts, is often easier, with a proper drop-down stainless-steel ladder bolted permanently in place, and a convenient cleat for the two painters on each corner of the transom.

Like every item of a boat's equipment, the simpler an operation of this kind can be made, the faster and probably safer it will be to carry out. Complicated performances (and we include in that the tying of unnecessary knots and undoing and doing-up of screw-type shackles where a clip would be quicker and better) can so easily go wrong – or are less likely to be attempted at all, when they should have been.

Baby lifejackets, etc.

We felt it worth investing (just in case) in a proper infant's lifejacket. Even the smallest kind of ordinary child's jacket is useless for tiny babies who are all the wrong shape to stay tied in when they start wriggling. However, there are fortunately one or two firms who make specialised baby flotation garments which not only stop a frightened occupant from accidentally struggling out, but also turn the wearer right end up and right way round, so that head and face are up out of the wet.

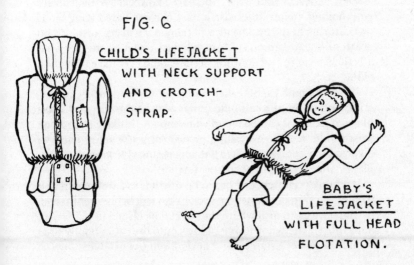

FIG. 6

CHILD'S LIFEJACKET
WITH NECK SUPPORT
AND CROTCH-
STRAP.

BABY'S
LIFEJACKET
WITH FULL HEAD
FLOTATION.

The sort we chose (we tested it in the bath, at home) had a buoyant hood padded with some kind of encapsulated foam. This not only provided flotation at the right end of the child, but gave it lovely soft protection in the event of contact with anything hard, in or out of the water. Each of our daughters wore this garment in turn, during their respective first season of boating.

One word about the buoyant filling of lifejackets for very young children. Foam-filled garments have an advantage over the sort with air-pockets or inflatable chambers; they can be chewed without the resultant puncturing destroying their effectiveness – and chewed they will almost certainly be.

Once aboard . . .

Having got infant and carrycot safely on board and below decks out of the wind, the important thing is to secure the child in the cot, and the cot in a safe place, where it won't fall about if the yacht heels over. Even in harbour this is advisable as a priority, if there is the remotest chance of the wash from a passing craft causing a sudden lurch or roll.

First choose a spot where the baby, however young, can see you moving about; otherwise it may become bored lying on its own, staring at the deckhead, whereupon it will cry, just for a bit of attention, and anxious Mum will dash down wondering what ails the wee mite and doubting if she should ever have brought it along, etc.

In very small yachts, such as trailer-sailers, pocket power-craft, and so on, the cabin floor may well be the best and safest place, if part of it can be found where no-one is likely to tread on or stumble over it. A cushion or two (or a few spare packs of disposable nappies) will be all that is required to keep the cot in place, since it can't then fall any further.

If a bunk is chosen, one has to be sure it is in a well-ventilated part of the ship, again where grown-ups can be frequently seen by the occupant, and where the cot can be lashed in place with light line. If the whole thing pitches onto the cabin floorboards from that sort of height, you'll never forgive yourselves.

So, having secured the cot, one must now make sure the baby is well wedged into that, maybe with rolled up cot blankets down the sides and round the foot area, because in a chop of a sea, the wee soul is otherwise likely to start sliding and rolling about on its plastic mattress, not knowing how to try and stop itself.

A hammock is sometimes better

We and others who have taken their babies boating, have eventually come to the conclusion that the Royal Navy of Yesteryear may have been right after all: so we rigged up a baby hammock.

One made of netting proved a mistake; little fingers and hands can get trapped in the mesh, and painfully bent, so we used canvas, as of old (well, Terylene sailcloth, actually, but it looked the same), and fitted a wooden cross-bar or 'stretcher' across the head and foot to ensure adequate spread. A flap of cloth stitched to the middle of one side and secured over the top to the other with tapes, is then all that is needed to ensure continuous occupancy, and the only thing to watch for is that there is no chance of it banging into anything as the ship rolls.

Babies love the sea

One of the first amazements we had when taking our firstborn sailing (on a brief cruise at the age of five weeks), was that the boat's motion seemed to delight and soothe her. The second was that it didn't make her seasick, for all our fears that it might. Only when all movement stopped, as we came to anchor in the total stillness of a tree-lined bay, did she give forth vocally with what was clearly a sense of deprivation.

It was not surprising, really: motion is both natural and comforting to a new-born baby. Everyone has seen mothers rocking a pram, a cradle, or a babe-in-arms. The motion of a boat underway saves all that effort, for it does the job automatically. Any sort of regular movement is agreeable: it is stillness that is boring. Put the carrycot in the back of the family car, and blissful silence will usually reward the driver for driving, but Heaven help all within earshot when the traffic lights go red or the journey comes to an end! So it is when at the end of the passage, a yacht is moored in a nice sheltered anchorage!

Maybe it can happen in exceptional cases, but we never have heard of a really tiny baby being seasick. They may of course 'blow back' after a feed or for some other reason, internal rather than external. Only when aged about two did any of our daughters experience seasickness for the first time, and we believe this to be the norm. Chapter 5, pages 98–102 discusses this at some length.

One of those chair things

There is rather a lot of gear associated with a baby, but one item we always felt worth having on board was a light plastic long-backed baby chair, which could be tied or clipped in a position where the infant could comfortably watch what was going on.

USEFUL INFANT CHAIR FOR BOATING.   FIG. 7

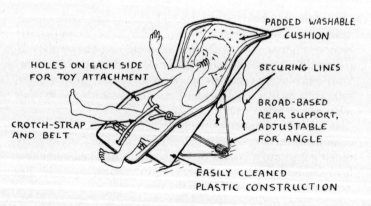

PADDED WASHABLE CUSHION

HOLES ON EACH SIDE FOR TOY ATTACHMENT

SECURING LINES

BROAD-BASED REAR SUPPORT, ADJUSTABLE FOR ANGLE

CROTCH-STRAP AND BELT

EASILY CLEANED PLASTIC CONSTRUCTION

The sort we used had its own seat-belt so that the child couldn't fall out.

The advantage was that it provided what must have been a welcome change of position, yet still supported the baby's head, and gave a much better view of the surroundings than was possible from the confines of a carrycot.

To do with nappies

We suspect there's something magic about how babies really get enough sustenance from their food; it seems that pretty well whatever you put in at one end comes to light in at least equal quantities at the other. And that is a problem parents (mothers usually) are unhappily faced with anywhere. Fortunately out at sea and far from land, it is one which is easier to deal with than it sometimes can be on shore.

For example, such items as disposable paper nappies, the kind which are bio-degradable and sink quite quickly, make the emptying of one's infants a simple matter, compared to dealing with the washable sort. (Mind you, we've read of one ocean-going family who swears by the latter, simply towing them on a line astern to clean them, and rinsing in a little fresh water afterwards, to remove the salt. We never tried it.)

Fortunately, as we all know, the ocean is a wonderful and productive waste-bin, and a few natural nutrients returned thereto from time to time do nothing but good (far enough offshore). If nothing else, gulls or fish will process them, and sea action will soon destroy the pads.

If land is close at hand, however, and especially if there is an on-shore breeze or current, disposable nappies are best collected in sealed polythene bags, to await a journey to the nearest suitable litter-bin (supposing Mum can't find a 'Ladies' with the appropriate receptacle).

The stowage of ready-to-use disposable nappies, particularly if one is embarking on a trip where the supply of such things may be a bit doubtful, can be something of a problem, in that they tend to be bulky. We found that since small children and babies take up very little room on a full-size adult bunk, we could often arrange for the packages of nappies to be stowed at one end – in the 'trotterbox' part, or tunnel end of the kind which extends under shelves or cockpit seats.

Ordinary washable nappies pose much more of a problem on coastal cruises, though stowage is less of a difficulty. Seawater does very well for washing them provided they really are very thoroughly rinsed in fresh to get rid of all the salt crystals (which apart from anything else are extremely abrasive on sensitive skin). The lifelines make superb clothes-lines, but you do require powerful clothes-pegs. The sort with a spring, or good old-fashioned wooden pegs are better than fancy modern clip-types, in that the breeze more often blows along the line than across it – at least when the boat is at anchor or on a free-swinging mooring.

Water and more water

Perhaps the greatest difficulty, both with washing nappies, and of course with washing baby-clothes and sometimes bedding, not to mention the baby itself, is an adequate supply of water. Gallons and gallons of the stuff are needed. We used to reckon that when Rona was very small, we used about 3 gallons (14 litres) *extra* water per day, and that was with disposable nappies. It all went on washing clothes, bathing her, sterilising bottles, and so on.

When Susan came along, Rona was less than a year-and-a-half older than her, and although requiring less frequent baths (a washdown mostly sufficing, as for the rest of us), she still caused the need for plenty of water for washing garments which had in one way or another come to grief.

Then Eileen arrived, not much more than a year after Sue, and we needed more water again. Clearly, large capacity main tanks in the cruising boat will help no end, but ours held only about 30 gallons (135 litres), and as we were often cruising in areas where the only supply for miles came from peaty lochs or from under a waterfall in a mountain burn, we used to supplement this with a number of 2-gallon (9-litre) plastic cans. At one time we had four or five of these stacked round the deck or down below.

We chose 2-gallon containers for the simple reason that one can walk quite a way with that amount in each hand, whereas a four or five gallon can, hung on the end of one arm is *murder* – as well as being more tricky and risky to lift aboard from the dinghy or lower down from high quaysides.

Inevitably, watering ship became a very regular routine, especially since we tended to top up wherever we got the chance. If alongside a quay and out of reach of a hose, we learned to take a suitable length of rope ashore with the cans, with which to lower them on our return.

Probably the best way to cut down on water consumption with babies on board is to cruise from launderette to launderette, though that of course rules out certain cruising areas.

Inflatabath

Bathing the baby is important, particularly in the early stages, to avoid nappy rash. We, with our relatively small yacht, looked at several rigid plastic baby baths, and wondered where ever we would stow such bulk. Then one day in a seaside town, our eyes lit upon a very small kiddy's inflatable 'dinghy' (in all less than 3ft long), no doubt intended for use without oars as a floating fun-thing in a shallow paddling pool, or alternatively as a minute paddling pool itself – but at any rate, obviously for the very, very young. It consisted of a single inflatable ring, highly colourful and approximately boat-shaped; the one we liked had a clear, transparent bottom. This last feature would be of interest in pools, whether paddling- or rock-type (and was to prove so in due course), but when we took it on board, inflated it, and placed it ready for the first bath conveniently on the cabin table, we did rather hesitate before pouring warm water onto what appeared (through it) to be the patterned tabletop.

It didn't melt – or have a 'blow out' – and proved a

marvellous solution to the whole problem, its bouncy sides being a great idea if the slippery baby started thrashing about. Since we were always as mean as possible about the amount of water we put in, the curve of the side-tube also helped prevent spills.

Bath-time wasn't always perfect though. There was one memorable occasion when a large speedboat came by unexpectedly close, and our little ship took one almighty roll just when Rona was in the pink and thoroughly soaped. The plastic bath took off, depositing bath and entire contents all over Mother. After that, we always put a damp skid-proof towel on the table before making the bath ready.

When the bath was finished with, it could be picked up, water and all, and emptied into the self-draining cockpit, which was then swilled down with a bucket of seawater. So was the bath, which was then hung up to dry. And very jolly it looked.

It lasted (with the odd patch) for all three of our children, and did many a turn among the shallows of a number of beaches as infants became toddlers and took an interest in underwater creatures. We deemed it very good value indeed, especially since once it was dry it could be quickly deflated, rolled up, and stowed unobtrusively on a narrow shelf.

When cruising is a milk-run

When it comes to babies in boats, mothers who breast-feed enjoy an advantage right from the start. Breast-feeding avoids all the tedium of sterilising bottles and teats, and of having to make up special powdered milk in the early stages, not to mention the difficulty of getting bottle and contents to just the right temperature before use. When you can't just plug in a proper electrical appliance for this purpose, it means heating water in a deep enough pan to warm the bottle, always supposing (when in a boat) that you have managed to fill the bottle in the first place in (perhaps) a jump of a sea.

As to sterilising the bottles afterwards, we used a rectangular, proprietary container which had a specially angled bottom, so that the bottles lay in the solution without air-bubbles, but it would also be possible to utilise a plastic food-box or ice-cream container, wedged at a suitable angle. A non-spill lid is of course vital, because most sterilising solutions are bleaches, and will fade practically anything other than plastic or glass.

Later on, obtaining cow or goat milk is a devilish problem in remote areas, and we found our three could always detect 'made up' milk of the powdered sort. It was usually necessary to have some as a stand-by. Only careful trial and error will eventually demonstrate which brand suits your family best, if 'real' milk is not available.

Here a medical word: before you set out on a cruise when the children are young, ask your family doctor if there are any special inoculations they should have. Milk in some places (even in the remoter parts of Britain) may not agree with children (or adults) brought up on the pasteurised, tuberculin-tested variety.

Night-feeds

When cruising, both mothers and fathers need all the sleep they can get, so if a very new baby is on board still requiring a night-time feed, daytime activities may have to be a little curtailed.

We found it easy enough to keep the *baby* warm while feeding it in the small hours. The main problem at that chilly hour is to keep Mother warm. A zip-fronted 'polar suit' of woolly, albeit synthetic, weave was the perfect answer, together with a pair of cosy slippers. Bottle-feeding does have this advantage, that parents can take it in turns, night and night about. Alas, where breast-feeding is concerned there is hardly much choice! And in those circumstances it helps if Father gets up and makes Mother a cup of tea, if only to lend a bit of moral support.

Although most babies will sleep anywhere and under almost any circumstances when they feel like it, when official bedtime came along, we used to try and make things a bit different, by drawing curtains in the fore-peak or wherever the baby was put for the night. We considered it well worth darkening the child's cabin like this, especially in high summer when on the West Coast of Scotland. On clear evenings, daylight there can hang around until practically midnight. This at least partial darkening of the sleeping cabin usually helped the little one to 'turn off' without much fuss.

You don't have to whisper!

Once when anchored in Strangford Lough in Northern Ireland, the crew of another yacht rowed over after supper for an evening's chat on board our little catamaran *Twintail*. And, as they say in that part of the world, 'the crack was very good'. We had been swapping yarns and laughing merrily for the best part of an hour before some remark of ours made the woman in the visiting crew realise we normally brought our children with us.

'Well, it's a good thing they aren't with you this trip, with the amount of din we're making,' she said.

'They're in their bunks right now,' we assured her.

'On board – *here?*' She lowered her voice and stared around the little saloon.

We pointed at the curtained-off entrances to the two quarter berths which extended under the cockpit seats, in each hull.

'Oh, good *heavens*!' she whispered 'We'd no idea! Why ever didn't you *say*? We'll have woken them up for sure . . .'

'Don't you believe it; they're quite used to noise,' we explained. 'Right from the start, we decided that they'd just have to get used to us chatting within earshot, or having the radio on. And they have. Look . . .'

Lifting aside one of the curtains, we revealed a tousled head of fair hair and a properly plugged in thumb – which one of us gently reached for and pulled away. The head never moved, nor did the long-lashed eyes open.

'What if something went wrong?'

Disapproving adults would often ask us what we'd do if the baby had a sudden health problem, and was it right anyway to take them afloat when it might be *hours* before we could get them ashore, if there was some kind of a crisis.

A Radio-Telephone would clearly be a grand thing to have on board, in that medical advice could be sought if the need arose. We in fact carried a simple emergency R/T set, but even if one had nothing of the sort, we see no reason why what we call 'local' cruises, over a weekend or two, might not be undertaken quite safely, where one spent most of the time at anchor or tied up close to base, and simply enjoyed living on board together, without shore-going pressures.

We were careful too to ensure that our infants were all reasonably healthy and in good form before we set out each time, and did not worry about the possibility of that awful misfortune of 'cot death' any more than we did at home; we felt that something like this was far more likely to go un-noticed until too late in the relatively large, multi-roomed space of a house, than when the child was virtually within arm's reach throughout the twenty-four hours in a little boat.

And as time passed, both of us began to feel that during these days afloat spent close together, we got to understand and 'read' the signs in a baby very much more quickly than during normal routine ashore.

As to our three infants, they in turn seemed to love the movement of yacht or dinghy, and their little eyes would instantly brighten at the call of a gull which, if it came into their field of view (usually only when we enticed them to catch crusts and breadcrumbs really close to the cockpit), would give cause for excited gurgling and thrashing about. And, no; they did not seem afraid of the big birds – they showed no fear on that account. The glitter of sunlit water especially, and the flapping of our brightly coloured ensign on its staff at the stern were things of the greatest fascination, also.

And from all that we have heard from other parents who like us took their babies boating at a very early age, it seems that the way our three took to it was both normal and natural.

4

Terrible Toddlers

Once a baby becomes active on its own account and starts crawling around, life afloat (and ashore) gets rather more complicated. For one thing, people aged only twelve or eighteen months generally have not the slightest sense of self-preservation, and will blissfully step into space, or put fingers or other parts into danger. The most important thing therefore is to restrain their movements without causing them discomfort, and to render the immediate environment as harmless to them as possible.

One really cannot make anywhere other than a padded cell truly safe, of course. Houses as we all know are awful traps for unsuspecting toddlers, and one might be forgiven for imagining that boats are a hundred times worse. In some respects the dangers may indeed be greater, and may certainly appear more obvious to the caring adult. The spaces involved, on the other hand, are smaller and in the cabin at least it may well prove easier than at home to arrange things safely.

When your baby is merely crawling, it's not so bad. Under supervision, it can be set down on the cabin floor, and so long as no-one treads on the little creature, and it can't get into the engine compartment, or trap fingers in low-level locker doors, quite a lot of 'steam' can usefully be run off at convenient times, even on wet days in port, by letting it explore unhindered. A nicely tired baby will go pleasantly to sleep with wondrous ease, and if the 'exercise period' is properly timed, just before Official Bedtime, the rewards will be ample for everyone.

Constant vigilance is needed

When they get to the stage of hauling themselves upright, one has really to watch out. That's when they have noticed how Mother sometimes twiddles those bright knobs on the front of the gas cooker, slides open locker doors, turns this thing, and pulls interestingly at that.

It comes as quite a shock the first time you find your explorative little one discovering on its own how cold (and salty) the water is at the bottom of the toilet pan.

A baby-chair of the kind with a built-in tray in front will prove worth its weight for those times when the child must be left unsupervised; the usual variety of toys can be piled before it, to be bashed, chewed, flung randomly about, and retrieved later. But in a boat the chair must be firmly secured, so that neither the child's rollicking nor any sudden lurch or roll can dislodge it.

Here is where one must begin to bear in mind the child's own human reaction, especially to anything puzzling or disturbing which it does not understand. We found it well worth while spending a moment before leaving our children alone in the cabin, explaining to them just what we'd be doing, and what they would see, hear, and probably feel as it happened. One doesn't want to blind the poor kid with incomprehensible science; a short sentence or two will probably cover most situations and leave the baby reassured.

As a result, when there are one or two thunderous bumps overhead and the boat starts vibrating to the flogging of a sail and suddenly appears (from below) to half fall over on its side, the child is neither alarmed nor particularly puzzled. And if ordinary adult nautical terms have been used, such as 'set sail' and 'heel over' small children seem able to work out the meaning of such boating terms as a matter of course. Indeed, as they grow, they rather tend to enjoy using the special language associated with boats and the sea, just as they relish particular favourite 'boaty' dishes which a sensible nautical mother will keep for use on board and avoids producing at home. (See the section on food, in Chapter 6.)

Danger down below

One can't keep even toddlers manacled to the baby-chair or strapped into a bunk for more than a while if they are awake and wanting to scramble about a bit, whether at sea or not, unless you have superbly efficient earplugs and a heart of ice. So during a two- or three-hour passage, they have to be allowed some moments when they can use their legs, unless it is obviously too rough. Curling up on the lee settee with Mum and a good storybook will seem a better idea anyway, in those conditions.

It is very difficult, as little ones learn to stand and walk about – especially in a boat where things to grab hold of are plentiful and at just the right height – for an adult to know how safe or otherwise their toddler really is on its pins. Development in the skill of standing and walking often comes with astonishing rapidity, and if protective arms are forever hovering around and getting in the way of the child's every independent movement, frustration will soon be audibly demonstrated. So, you have to let them go now and then – which, of course, is when they fall.

Our catamaran heeled seldom more than a few degrees, but in a lurch of a sea, as the children began to be 'mobile' below decks, there was considerable danger of one or other of them falling down from the saloon level on the bridgedeck, into one or other of the hulls, several feet below. Tethering them so that they couldn't, by means of their walking harnesses (which we converted into sea-going safety harnesses, as described on page 69), worked quite well, but sooner or later when one wasn't expecting it, the harness wasn't on and a sudden lurch, perhaps at anchor and caused by a passing boat, would catch one of them in just the wrong spot – with the inevitable result.

Fence them in!

On deck, a set of guardrails (lifelines) is vital even on the tiniest of cruisers, if toddlers or the not-much-older are liable to want freedom to clamber about. (See Chapter 2, pp. 34–5.) Netting can be added to close the gaps between the lines, and is no doubt the best answer from a safety point of view, but it can make the handling of mooring warps and sometimes headsail sheets very awkward, and to our eyes anyway, looks *awful*.

In our own boats we preferred to make do with our pre-stretched Terylene lifelines and stanchions, and to insist that the children were only allowed on deck, when under way, if wearing properly secured safety-harnesses. In port, or at anchor, lifejackets would suffice, after the age of two. Thus from the start, they came to understand and be fully aware of the risks of going overboard; and until they were much older and competent swimmers, they never did.

Round off the corners

We did have one quite serious accident, when for some reason Susan – often accident-prone – was not in her straps. We were under way in fairly sheltered water, when a particularly steep little wave caught the boat awkwardly beam-on. Sue had been standing, looking out of the window and holding onto the end of one of the settees, right at the top of the steps leading down into the port hull. Some sort of squabble was going on between her sisters, and no-one was watching her when the lurch came. There was a thud and a short and ominous silence, producing instant consternation among her parents. At least the ear-shattering screech which followed told us that she wasn't unconscious – and indicated where she had vanished to. We found her lying in a very sorry little heap at the foot of the steps with a hefty swelling appearing on her forehead and a certain amount of blood making it even more dramatic.

She would not have been particularly hurt had it not been for the fact that her head had struck a corner of the chart-table, but there was a cut to deal with, as well as the rising bump. It was one of many occasions when we blessed a well-stocked First Aid kit and some small knowledge of how to cope.

And we need hardly say that the skipper spent that evening and most of the next morning doing what he should have done long before, namely taking a rasp, plane, and sandpaper, and rounding every edge and projecting corner and angle in the ship. It was worth it too, because Eileen later took a tumble in much the same way – and got no more than a nasty bruise from that same corner of the chart-table.

Why didn't we put a 'gate' of some kind at the top of those steps down into the hull? For one thing such an obstruction would have made it very awkward to move about the catamaran, and for another, we felt – and still feel even more strongly – that being too thoroughly protective is not always best in the long run, for the child concerned. If a child is *never* allowed to fall or bump itself, it will *never* know to be careful not to – until it has grown to a size when its greater weight and more brittle bones result in far worse and perhaps lasting injury. When they are light and have fairly rubbery bones, such lessons can be learned in relative safety, and *in good time*.

Think 'safety' – because the children won't!

The main thing is for parents to see to it that any likely falls or other potential dangers are not going to cause permanent hurt.

On deck, sheet blocks and long hair should be kept well away from each other. Indeed *no* straggly hair should be allowed near *any* rotating machinery. Below, one thinks immediately of those risks associated with the cooking appliances. Children can be unfortunately observant in some ways, and will certainly have seen how their mother does things with the cooker controls. (These, in a boat, are often at a height which an inquisitive two-year-old can just about reach.)

For this reason, the cook has to be scrupulous about *always* turning off the gas supply as a matter of routine at the end of each meal or hot drink prepared – and about checking that all the gas taps are still in the 'off' position before turning the supply back 'on', for the next cooking session.

Most gas cookers nowadays have so-called 'child-proof' taps, which you have to push in before turning, but as we found more than once, children can notice how you do that, too! And you needn't think (as we did) that you'll be safe with pressure-paraffin cookers and cabin-heaters, not unless you can honestly be bothered always to release the entire tankful of pressure between sessions. The sweat of pumping back up to full pressure for vaporising each time is considerable, and we found that little fingers can turn the burner control knobs and gently flood the whole galley with nice smelly, slippery paraffin . . . There are meths burners, of course, but they cook much more slowly; and methylated spirits can be tricky stuff to have around.

While we're on the subject of potential catastrophes, saucepan handles left sticking out over the edge of the cooker can be an appalling danger afloat as at home. The fiddle on a boat's cooker-top may stop the pan itself being pulled over, but won't prevent its hot contents from being tipped out, so the habit of always turning the pan-handles round so that they cannot be grabbed from in front is best cultivated right from the start. That may be easier for Mother, assuming that she does most of the cooking. The big risk comes when Father – or some other adult – goes down to make the Mate a nice cup of cocoa, and forgets to be so careful.

Up on deck – hoods, tents and dodgers

As already explained, kids need fresh air and plenty of it, and so long as they are insulated from the chilling effect of cold winds and/or the burning rays of strong sunlight, time spent in the cockpit both at sea and in port will usually prove beneficial both to their bodily health and to their mental alertness.

That chair (p. 63), with the tray in front and a set of shoulder straps like a racing-driver's safety harness can be used here to great effect, if it can be lashed into a safe corner, out of danger from flailing ropes, etc.

A hood-type canopy or other form of sheltering barrier, rigged over the front of the cockpit completes the picture, providing shelter not just at sea, but when lying at anchor with the ship head to wind (see p. 35).

We found a large cockpit tent particularly useful when our girls were small, and we were cooped up in harbour by strong winds and rain – which was pretty often, because we soon discovered that it doesn't pay to be underway for more than an hour or two if you can help it, in those conditions, when the children are on board.

Our tent extended over the boom and down to the guardrails on either side, where a set of clips on short lengths of elastic shock-cord made it quick to secure or remove. In length, it stretched from ahead of the cabin hatchway, right back to the rear end of the cockpit, where either corner could be rolled up and tied back out of the way, to facilitate access. The front could be closed off completely, like the door end of a 'land' tent, so that the sliding hatch could be left wide open in the wettest weather, to give extra light and air in the cabin. Actually, from this point of view, we often thought we might have been better off with a tent made from reinforced translucent plastic sheeting – ours was a converted trailer cover made of rather heavy proofed canvas.

The big snag with a cockpit tent of any kind is that it is just one more bulky thing to stow. Depending on its shape and size, it may also make the boat sheer about a good deal when she's at anchor in a blow. But there's another thing to consider. Some easy means of getting rid of it in a hurry is imperative, if only because a situation may arise unexpectedly, making it vital to get under way with the utmost rapidity.

Weathercloths in the lifelines abreast the cockpit also help to keep down draughts and unexpected dollops of spray; but they do rather restrict the view. From the child's low eye-level, they therefore rule out anything of interest much beyond what is in the cockpit itself. This drawback has to be weighed against the extra protection which weathercloths provide if a small person gets caught off-balance and is thrown towards the lifelines . . .

This brings us to the next problem, which is that of generally keeping little crawlers and toddlers on board.

Strict rules from the outset

As our three in turn got to the crawling age, they were also on the point of growing out of the baby lifejackets, and yet were too small for any then-available 'child'-size lifejacket. So we were pretty well forced into what was anyway the best safety precaution at that age: we tethered them.

First we made a Ship's Rule, which we firmly impressed on everyone on board, including the children, to the effect that the children were never to be allowed on deck while the yacht was under way unless wearing a safety-harness. The exceptions would be (a) when at anchor or in harbour, when a properly tied-on lifejacket would suffice, (b) when under the cockpit tent in the presence of an adult, and (c) when we were about to take them ashore, and in that case the most appropriate size of lifejacket had to be donned, as carefully as possible, instead.

At the ends of their tethers . . .

No-one in those days made a proper safety-harness of a boating type to fit the under-twos, and even now the smallest we have seen is rather big, stiff and awkward, and extremely expensive.

So we made a set of our own from a good-quality 'toddler's walking harness', which had strong synthetic webbing straps and good jamming buckles, so that it could be adjusted to be fairly high up around the chest. Our one important modification allowed the safety-line to be attached in front, so that if the child ever did reach the water, it would automatically be rotated and lifted so that face and shoulders were uppermost. (The walking reins unclipped anyway, so they were no problem.) We also thought a crotch strap a good idea, and made one from the reins, that being the same material as the rest of it.

Any such harness must of course have sufficient strength not to fail, should the child's weight come on suddenly, and the line securing it – and thus your child – to the ship, along with any clips or fastenings, should of course be equally up to that same jerk-strain.

It is a curious fact, but once human children reach the age of standing on their own two little feet and leaning over things, *they are ridiculously top-heavy*. The arms, chest, and particularly the head are much larger and heavier than the legs at that young age. Thus tripping, falling, and general over-balancing are all-too-common experiences.

'What if they fall overboard?'

Yes, well – apart from securing the safety-harness line to the right part of the child, thought has to be given to where to make it fast on the ship. We used a securing point near the centreline of the boat when the kids were in the cockpit, adjusting the length of the line so that while each child had plenty of scope to move around, none of them could actually reach the water, even supposing they accidentally tripped up right out on the sidedeck. In other words we arranged the line to go tight – at the latest – as the child reached the rail.

FIG. 8

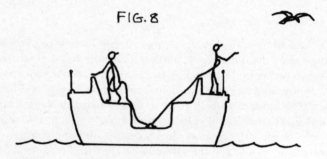

SAFETY–HARNESSES ATTACHED
NEAR YACHT'S CENTRE–LINE
AFFORD SAFETY WITHOUT UNDUE
RESTRAINT.

This way they could stand holding onto the lifelines and watching things happening outside the ship. When they did fall, while bits of them could go partly out under the lower lifeline, they would stop well short of actually getting wet. This scheme seemed to work particularly well, in that it apparently gave them a proper respect for the dangers of going overboard the first time each of them (inevitably) fell there, and was confronted with a sudden view of the dark water lapping close below them. And years later, long after harness-wearing became a matter for open-water use only, not one of them ever fell overboard. The extreme risk safely learned and understood in early childhood still made them careful on that account. One or two of them have since done the usual trick of inadvertently disappearing 'twixt ship and dinghy when fooling about as strong-swimming teenagers, but that's a different matter!

The important point is that had they *never* been able to get near the boat's side as toddlers, the appreciation of this greatest of boating hazards – falling overboard – might not have sunk in enough; later on numerous, and possibly dangerous, duckings might have resulted simply from a lack of awareness of how easily it can happen.

Netting versus harnesses

As already mentioned, many parents prefer to rig netting around the yacht's lifelines, so that there is never a chance of the child slipping overboard (unless it is daft enough to climb over). We ourselves considered the use of netting several times, but always came back to the thought that where the extremely young are concerned, it would be better simply not to allow them out of the cockpit *at all* when the yacht was under way, other than in exceptionally calm conditions and with an adult holding on to some part of them. Possibly had we rigged netting all round, we might not have felt this particular restriction was quite as necessary.

The trouble is there are so many dangers on the deck of a sailing boat – and on motor boats too. There are lots of things to trip over in the way of deck-fittings, mooring cleats, and so on. Where there are sails, there is the possibility of a flick from the sheet of a flogging headsail, and little feet can slip violently on even a small-diameter rope lying slack along the sidedeck.

The height of lifelines, netted or otherwise, can appear to be sufficient, except that even kids who don't look anything like tall enough to tip over the top of them, may nevertheless manage to do so because of that in-built top-heaviness which we mentioned earlier.

All in all, we decided to permit toddlers' visits to the deck outside the cockpit only under attentive supervision, and always with that safety-harness firmly attached. When they were very tiny, we went to considerable lengths to ensure that they were always watched even when in the confines of the cockpit. Yet, kids being what they are, we still had the odd appalling fright. One occasion in particular sticks vividly in our memories, and may serve to drive home the importance of such supervision.

Twintail, our first little cruising cat, was anchored one sunny morning close under the pine-trees of a totally calm and gloriously steep-sided Scottish loch. Down below, the skipper was checking his charts in preparation for a possible drift round to the next anchorage that afternoon, and Rona and Susan, our eldest two, were for once playing peacefully together at the cabin table. The mate had been in the cockpit, shelling peas for lunch, and chatting to Brian, our teenaged crew, who in turn was amusing thirteen-month-old Eileen, and at the same time watching birds with the ship's binoculars.

It should be explained that Eileen had long been crawling with great verve, but had only a few days before during this very cruise, taken her first unaided proper steps, making a succession of mad rushes across the five-foot-wide cockpit, from person to person. However, she still preferred clambering and climbing over seats, steps, and people.

As usual, being in the cockpit, she was wearing her harness, with its rope adjusted to let her just reach the rail on either side.

'Keep an eye on her, Brian,' said the mate. 'I'm just going below to put the peas on to cook.' And she stepped down into the galley on the starboard side. After putting the peas in a saucepan of water and lighting the stove, she went out again, and at once cried 'Oh-my-God! Where is she?'

This brought the skipper on deck in one movement, and the two of us stared about the cockpit, where only an astonished Brian could be seen – and a taut harness safety-line stretching from its point of attachment, back over the top of the two-foot high transom between the boat's stubby sterns. And there it disappeared downwards.

We dived aft with intakes of breath.

Eileen, however, was not dangling in the drink, but sitting

contentedly at the full extent of the line, on the timber floor of the big outboard bracket, carefully inspecting one of her toy boats which the skipper had stowed there the previous evening. Her totally disarming smile as she looked up at us, left us floundering helplessly.

Though we knew she couldn't reach the water, not being able to see her at all for a moment had been quite a shock, and brought home to all of us how silently and suddenly a child *could* come to grief. Poor Brian, with his eyes glued to the binoculars and a distant heron, had heard nothing despite being within four feet of her – we suspect because young Eileen had known very well she was up to a bit of mischief, and had contrived to achieve her aim without a sound.

And that, of course, is too often the beginnings of innocent but highly dangerous escapades where the very young are concerned.

Harness tracks

Both for adult and junior crew-members, we fitted our boat with tracks along the tops of the cabintop handrails, with a couple of slides in each, to take safety-harness clips. Thus we could clip on our harnesses whilst still safely in the cockpit, go forward dragging the clips and lines after us, and get to within reach of the forestay for changing jibs, etc., without ever having to unclip. Clearly the lead of the mast shrouds will decide whether this is a possible arrangement in your boat – that, and the length and profile of the coachroof. But normally, a wire or some other sort of jackstay system for harness lines can be rigged without too much difficulty, and it's certainly worth it. Having to move only a few feet at a time in a real jump of a sea, then having to stop and unclip, reach forward to another safety point, and clip on again before gaining another yard is a poor and tedious and none-too-safe means of progression even for adults; it is even more risky for children to try.

Another idea we found useful in this connection was to fit our harness lines with a second hook, part way along the line. This, when snapped into the D-ring on the harness belt itself, shortened the line to a safer length while one was for instance on the way forward or aft again. It could be released as one attained one's objective, to allow further scope (as when reefing the mains'l), but at all times one remained secured to the ship.

Shore-going with lifejackets

Young children should always be made to wear lifejackets, preferably the sort with neck support, even when accompanying their parents along marina pontoons, or on quaysides, jetties, riverbanks, or canal locks. Far too many tragedies have occurred through kids frisking about and over-balancing near the edge. Once in the water, sheer panic often results in total inability to swim or climb out. The wearing of a properly secured lifejacket of the right size may do nothing to prevent such a fall, but with luck the effect will be no more than a wetting and a severe but maybe salutary fright.

In the dinghy, or in any really small craft such as a speedboat, we all know that *everyone* should wear a lifejacket, all the time. In practice, however, there are often a number of apparent 'reasons' for not doing so – as for instance when rowing ashore for a restaurant meal, when one would hardly wish to arrive with armfuls of bulky, brightly-coloured flotation garments for each member of the crew. What often happens, in all but the most careful families, is that those who are proven swimmers do not bother with lifejackets, unless the trip betwixt ship and shore is obviously going to be hazardous. (And where some adult crews are concerned, the return from an evening ashore can be hazardous enough for anyone, even in a flat calm.)

Wise parents will realise that if *they* themselves wear buoyancy garments each time they use the dinghy, their children will grow up accepting this as a normal and seamanlike precaution, with nothing 'cissy' about it.

We used to take ashore with us a couple of small and reasonably smart-looking sailbags or folding knapsacks, into which our safety gear could be stuffed on arrival. These were light to carry, and not an embarrassment in public places. They also held a fair amount of other things, like a spare nappy or two, oilskin trousers, beach things, and on the return journey could be used for the proceeds of our shopping expeditions.

On the journey back out to the yacht with the dinghy well laden, small children will generally be quite content to sit beside their mother, while Father rows or operates the outboard engine, but from the start, strict dinghy discipline is essential. The young must be firmly made to sit *still*, emphasising that this is for the safety of the boat and everyone in it, and that it also makes the job of rowing easier. This way the child can begin to feel that he is doing his bit as part of the boat's crew.

'Fingers inboard!'

The most important thing to watch out for, as you approach the yacht (or jetty, etc.), are those tiny fingers clutching the gunwale. They can so easily be forgotten, and may get severely nipped or crushed as the dinghy comes alongside. It is little use expecting the very young to foresee what is going to happen, nor to remember for themselves to keep their hands inboard, especially since 'holding on carefully' is what they are being asked to do.

Children generally think only of the immediate present, and seldom even try to anticipate dangers like this, or any kind of consequence of actions which to them seem perfectly natural and sensible.

So it is up to the adults to be on the lookout for things like this,

FIG. 9

"FINGERS INBOARD!"

DANGER !

on behalf of their offspring, and a routine call of 'Fingers inboard!' at the appropriate moment each time the family dinghy comes alongside, will soon become part of the occasion.

Trailing toy boats

Towing toy boats from the dinghy – or from the parent vessel – can be fascinating for children with the right imaginative temperament, and can keep them engrossed and quiet for considerable periods. Our three used to experiment with an assortment of buoyant (or less than buoyant) objects which when trailed astern at different speeds either behaved like little powerboats, or hopped and skipped, or simply wobbled curiously just beneath the surface in our wake (see pp. 133–4).

Fine fun, except that again there must be safety rules, especially when an outboard engine (or one with the propeller anywhere near the surface) is in use. The tow-line, however easily breakable, should never be looped round the child's wrist, or tied to him/her in any way, lest it gets caught in the machinery and suddenly wound in. The child will never think of this for itself; it is for the parent to point it out – and then Make The Rule.

We always tied the inboard end of such lines to some part of the towing craft – a dinghy thwart, or the base of a guardrail stanchion – so that the child could handle the line in safety, so long as it didn't actually wrap it around its hand or fingers at any time. It also had the advantage that they could let go, without there being an immediate howl for Daddy to 'turn the boat round' and go back for the released article.

Hot weather games

The risks and remedies associated with sunburn and heat-stroke will be dealt with in Chapter 5, and a number of assorted games and amusements in Chapter 7, but it is worth mentioning here how much fun young children can have in warm weather with a simple thing like a bucket of water on the cockpit floor.

If the bucket is at all full, and the child *very* small, supervision will of course be needed, but the splashing and experimenting with floating toys will keep little kids happy for ages. Something from which to pour water (however bizarre), and one or two floatable oddments provide endless interest.

Our inflatable baby-bath (Chapter 3, pp. 57–8) would often come into use as a paddling pool in our catamaran's relatively large cockpit. If its transparent plastic bottom was put down on a sheet of black polythene in full sunlight, ice-cold seawater, poured in to a depth of a couple of inches, heated up by solar energy in twenty minutes or so, and provided many a 'swim' when a sandy beach was not to hand.

'*S–a–n–d*'

In taking their young children boating, and in particular taking them cruising for several days at a stretch, parents have to accept the fact that the actual business of boating, by which we mean the time spent under way, will be of far more interest to themselves than to their kids. Toddlers especially tend to accept their environment merely as a fact of life, and the family boat to them may mean no more than a very slow vehicle which can be made to transport them from one beach to the next.

As the children's distance vision grows more of interest to them, unless Father wants to be continually hounded into stopping off at every bit of sand visible during a coastal passage between two ports of call, mention of the stuff amongst adults must either be avoided, or coded, in order to spare the junior crew undue disappointments.

Beaches, though plentiful in some coastal areas, are never all that common, and are often in hopelessly exposed and dangerous places from the mariner's point of view, however enticing they might appear to those who adore such features. All the same, we used to note the locations of any likely-looking strips of sand when passing to and fro on our normal cruising holidays, logging them for perhaps future occasions when time, tide, and the right wind direction, *and* a sunny day, might coincide. Then we could have no hesitation in making a worthwhile visit there, to appease and delight our brood.

'Bit of sand there,' we would say to each other, until the time when such remarks brought forth an instant chorus of 'Can we go there, Daddy? Please, Daddy, please?' So we got into the way of surreptitiously spelling the word.

In the end, it all came back to explaining to them how putting in would in the present onshore wind, be really dangerous. Our explanation worked just so long as that really was the case, because we found that they could follow the reasoning, if it had been simply presented to them, at an amazingly early age. They were soon asking not so much 'can we?' as 'would it be safe to?'. We think that most cruising parents will find time spent anchored off some suitable sandy beach, while even one of them goes ashore with the kids for an hour or two, extremely rewarding.

Beaches are the very best places for the young to let off steam, especially after a day or two of being cooped up on board in the cramped confines of a small boat, when they will probably have become somewhat fractious and irritable. An afternoon spent romping in the soft sand above the tide-line, or splashing about in the shallows, will expend masses of pent-up energy. (Bearing in mind the risks of cuts from broken bottles, etc., if it's that sort of beach.)

The greatest difficulty, from the skipper's point of view, arises from the fact that by their very nature, the majority of sandy beaches are on exposed coastlines, where shells and stones washed up from the seabed over the ages have been ground into tiny granules by the action of heavy surf. No seaman likes anchoring on a lee shore for a start, so unless the wind is light and off-shore, it is crazy to leave the yacht unattended, even though you might be in sight of her all the time.

The other problem comes when there is even a small amount of surf rolling onto the shore, for landing by dinghy then becomes exceedingly risky. If it is to be attempted, the beach should first be studied carefully with binoculars from as high a sight-line as possible, to see where the least disturbed part lies.

The higher you can get to carry out such a search the better. In *Twintail* we rigged ratlines in the lower shrouds for this very purpose, though with the simple rigging of many modern yachts, a good set of mast-steps, the sort permanently attached to the mast, will often have to suffice.

Beaching the dinghy

Having spotted the least troubled corner of the beach, one should take the yacht in as close as the fall of the tide will permit, and as near to that part of the shore as possible. As this is likely to be towards a corner near rocks, on some coasts, it goes without saying that this should be done slowly and with someone in the bows, and with the sounder being carefully watched. Distances can be awfully deceptive on the water. We have frequently brought our little ship in and in towards such a beach or cove, anchoring when we thought we could practically walk ashore, only to discover we had before us a very long row to get in – and what seemed like a very much longer one to get back out to her again!

Lifejackets should be donned by everyone in the shore-party, *even if they intend to swim*. If the dinghy should get out of control and tip everyone out in the surf, it is important that in the case of someone being winded or otherwise hurt, they should automatically float face-up, even in a foot or two of water.

The best approach will largely depend on the circumstances, and to some extent on the type of dinghy, an inflatable usually being better for this sort of thing than a rigid boat. Above all, full buoyancy, enough to support all in the boat when swamped, is vital. Keeping the boat end-on to the breakers is essential all the way in, and there is much to be said for going in stern-first, so that the oarsman can use his paddles as brakes. Dinghy bows are intended to 'meet' broken water; transoms are not, so if the stern is presented to a curling wave-top, swamping is likely to occur. If much water is shipped in this way, many dinghies tend to lose stability.

If one has been able to anchor the parent ship close enough, and has sufficient rope for the purpose, a good method of keeping control is to veer the dinghy in to the shore on the end of a warp – which can then be used to retrieve it and its occupants in due course. One should of course allow for what happens as the tide comes in over the sand.

Don't forget that if using a beach in an offshore wind (which is after all the only safe time to do so), the dinghy must be carried well clear of the water when you arrive, or the rising tide, a puff of wind, or the swirl of a larger wave than expected, may remove it when you aren't looking.

Another dinghy law not to forget is: the dinghy should have its own anchor and its own bailer secured to it, especially if children are to use it as their own boat.

Take ashore a packet of assorted First Aid plasters, and some disinfectant. Cuts, whether from broken glass, sharp-edged shells, or merely abrasive rocks are all too commonly experienced, even on the most remote of beaches, and it can take quite a few minutes to row a frightened and bleeding child back out to the ship.

When they get older, beach bonfires and 'sausage-sizzles', and games with 'Frizbees', kites, and other things (see Chapter 6, p. 123 and Chapter 7, p. 134) will be popular. So will swimming, but the thing that makes it so very worth while from the parent's point of view (quite apart from that of the children) will be that youthful energy is thus expended.

If during such an afternoon excursion, the parents themselves have been able to laze about, either while supervising on shore, or keeping anchor-watch on the waiting boat, the moment when the children are back on board, fed, and put to bed, might be the best time to set out on a night passage of some distance – no doubt to spend a further day in similar fashion on some other, perhaps foreign, beach, but well on your way.

Night passages

When the children are very young, almost the only way to manage a passage expected to last more than eight hours or so, without them becoming bored through being cooped up in

1. Writing a 'running letter' to post at the next port of call.

2. 'Don't forget your lifejacket!' Three families going afloat in suitable dinghies: l. to r. – a GP14, a 14ft Skipper, and an Enterprise.

3. 'Can I steer, Daddy?'

4. Just some of the items for an infant passenger: Carrycot, infant armchair, babychair with tray and set of wheels, vacuum flask, sterilizing liquid and container with spare bottles, disposable nappies, baby powder, cup, spoon, puree-maker, 4-gallon water container, inflatable baby-bath (play-pool), towels, nylon suit, lifejacket, soft toy, and boathook for quick retrieval of whatever goes overboard!

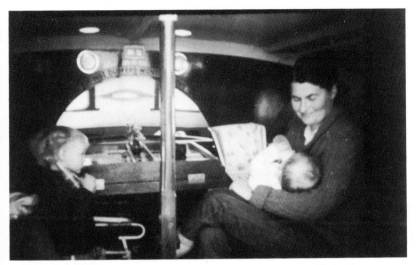

5. Night feed on board the authors' 27ft catamaran *Twintail*.

6. Leaving the cockpit safely, with harness clipped into slide in
a track on the cabintop handrail.

7. Helping on deck . . .

8. A wild moment in a game of 'dinghy tig'.

harnesses or below decks, is to do it while they sleep. So a Channel crossing of say 10 or 12 hours' duration is maybe best attempted at night.

If the skipper at least can manage a bit of a snooze after lunch, he can get the yacht under way after supper, while the kids are being bedded down. Then, when Mother has time to take over, there may still be plenty of daylight left to let you both settle into a proper watch-keeping routine before night-fall.

Many families use a 'two on, two off' watch system when only two adults are on board. This means little more than cat-napping during the two hours spent off-watch, when a saloon or quarter berth will be invaluable. We ourselves did not very often sail at night, because once on our favourite cruising ground among Hebridean waters, ports of refuge were so plentiful; but whenever we did so, we thought a better system was based on 2½ hours 'on'. (Three hours at a stretch always seemed too long.) We reckoned that for the first half-hour one was getting the feel of the helm and the seas in the dark, and generally settling down, and for the next hour-and-a-half one could relax and enjoy the experience – with any luck. One was only just beginning to feel fed up and longing for one's bunk by the time the final half-hour came to an end.

Not perhaps being used to watch-keeping at night, many parents who do so only once or twice in the year may find it hard to get to sleep when below decks under way. Fathers in particular, who do most of the sailing during the day, may well find they aren't all that familiar with the very different sounds of the ship's progress as heard through the thickness of the hull. A degree of nervousness, to do with the dark and feelings of responsibility to one's family when crossing shipping lanes, etc., do nothing to induce sleep, and the first forty minutes, or even the first hour or so off-watch, is often spent mentally fussing, while lying wide awake in the dark and reeling cabin.

A two-hour watch below, when one needs time at each end of it to get out of and back into oilskins and boots, let alone brew a hot drink to share at the change-over, often leaves time for little more than a perfunctory doze. It is worse still in the 'wee small hours', if one has only just sunk into deep slumber with one's body temperature lowered, when the dreaded call of 'Hey! Your watch!' drags you back to consciousness. So that extra half-hour in the 2½-hour system can make a world of difference to one's ability to rest properly and then to remain awake when on deck.

Another hand

If of course one can take along an experienced adult friend who doesn't mind the noise and other aspects involved in living in very close proximity to tiny children, it will enable the parents to get a lot more rest and relaxation during a boating holiday.

With a 'third hand', even a two-hour watch system will mean each individual having four hours at a stretch off-watch below decks, during night passages. On a twelve-hour crossing, this makes a marvellous difference, each person taking over only twice. With the 2½-hour plan, 'three-up' on the same length of a trip, one of the adults involved need only do one watch 'on'. It seems only right that this person should be Mother, rather than Father or the crew, on the basis that she probably has had, and is going to have, a more tiring day (with the children) than either of the others.

Having a third adult on board when the kids were very small solved another problem which we somehow hadn't thought of in advance. Not only did the skipper not have to rely on Mother being able to lend a hand at crucial moments (we explained earlier on, the crises that happen the moment she is required on entering or leaving port, etc.), but when in harbour, at least once or twice during a fortnight's cruise, the third person could perhaps stay on board and baby-sit, while the parents could get ashore for a meal on their own. This luxury, when we were normally so very closely tied to the kids in the first years, for us turned the cruise into a very real holiday experience.

If your boat is too small to accommodate an extra adult, the only way you can get free to dine ashore without the kids, is to persuade some kindly crew from another boat to baby-sit for you, reciprocating afterwards with some suitable gift or indeed a similar service – but obviously you would not only have to find someone you can be sure about, but one who will be capable of doing the right thing with the boat should some nautical situation crop up in your absence.

One final word on night-passages; whether you have an extra hand or not, when the night is over, and you arrive at your destination around breakfast-time, tired, and all ready to turn in to your bunk after being up, or at best having slept only fitfully most of the night, that is when your chirpy, fully-rested little offspring bounce awake, demanding to be fed, amused, and taken ashore to that beach you failed to notice you'd anchored off.

There is no known answer to this one!

Early to bed, early to rise

Because of the conflict of the differing active periods of adults and children in the ordinary way, the adults on board may find their own day less of a strain if they adjust their times of waking and sleeping to be more in line with those of their children. In average shore-based life-styles, this does not work too well at home, but afloat we found there were distinct advantages. For one thing, waking in time to hear the morning shipping forecast (often surprisingly different from the late-night forecast, some six hours earlier) lets one plan the day's sailing or shore-going more satisfactorily and successfully to meet expected weather conditions, than banking on what you sleepily listened to the night before.

'Silence, please . . .'

One Ship's Rule we absolutely insisted on from the start was to have total silence amongst those on board while the forecast was being taken down (radio reception sometimes being less than perfect), and the children soon learned to shut up without being told when the familiar 'Here is the Shipping Forecast' came on the air.

Breakfast can be made while the children are still stirring, and everyone starts the day together. Working to this sort of routine, we were often under way and enjoying perfect sailing conditions before eight o'clock, and had made a satisfactory passage to the next anchorage or port of call (or beach) before noon.

Quite a number of families we have spoken to find that with a longish passage before them, making a very early start, say about 0430 (depending on tides, etc.), and leaving the children asleep in their bunks until their normal breakfast-time, works well. It certainly did whenever we tried it, and one seems to arrive at the destination fresher that way than after a full night crossing.

Parental relaxation

We very soon learned to shorten our sailing day, anyway, turning into our bunks often around nine or half-past, and getting up about six-thirty, which was when the kids normally became vocal. (There was never much point in trying to keep them quiet once they had decided it was daytime!)

We also cut down on sea-time, planning our more modest passage-making in order to have the hook down by about five-thirty in the afternoon at the latest, most days. Supper could then be enjoyed 'en famille', and once the bedtime routine was complete, our children soon realised that they should allow the next two hours for parental relaxation. (By the end of which, if not long before, they were fast asleep, even if we weren't.)

So, after our evening noggin together in the cockpit (weather permitting), the skipper would write up the day's log, while the mate would maybe indulge in her favourite pleasure and row off solo in the dinghy to explore the anchorage, or drift dreamily over the shallows, watching sea-creatures or enjoying the swooping flight of terns, or the still patience of a heron fishing for his supper. Putting a bit of distance between herself and the children for even half an hour or so each day like that, proved entirely a Good Thing – just so long as she knew someone was left on board to baby-sit.

Those relatively peaceful moments after the kids were bedded down were invaluable. A mother gets if anything even more closely involved with small children in the enclosed confines of a yacht than she would at home, and she also has to contend with the constant motion of the craft and still keep going throughout the day, with all the usual jobs.

The boating father also requires plenty of rest, because he will have had to manage much if not most of the sailing and general deck-work on his own, while his wife tends the young. More importantly he, as Skipper, will almost certainly feel he carries ultimately 'all the responsibility', a term which now that he has children, goes very deep indeed. And that in itself is surprisingly wearing. Unless he is a most unusual father, he, like Mother, will benefit greatly from at least a short time each day without the clamour of kids about him and the constant need to keep a guardian eye on them while they play around the ship.

Pets

The above almost equally applies to families who bring their household pet sailing; short passages between ports, and diligent, watchful care of dogs or cats are just as necessary as with children.

One has to decide, perhaps after experiment, whether it is really fair to the animals concerned (and the accompanying humans) to bring them along, especially for more than the odd day at a time. A house-trained dog, for example, may suffer a great deal in the effort to contain itself over a long period at sea, rather than make a mess in what it rightly regards as an extension of its master's home. (Cats can usually be trained to use a sand-tray, but are more likely to stray ashore in strange ports.) And there are serious complications of anti-Rabies laws to obey if one is 'going foreign' and/or coming back to Britain.

We decided against taking animals cruising, though our parakeets, Port and Starbird, seemed to enjoy the experience. Not all cage-birds might be robust enough to withstand the marked temperature changes encountered on board a yacht.

5

'The Healthy Sport'

Boating is generally accepted as being among the very healthiest of sports imaginable, but when children are on board the normal childish health problems are bound to arise from time to time.

There is no point here in trying to itemise all possible ailments, nor the many proprietary remedies for this and that which one *could* (in a large enough yacht) carry on board. What we do recommend is that you get yourself a copy of a good, clear book on the subject, such as *The Illustrated Family Medical Encyclopaedia*, a large but invaluable tome published by The Reader's Digest Association.

Having good basic information on board with you will be appreciated for the way it tells plainly how to cope with minor injuries; or it may simply reassure you that an apparent problem is nothing serious, or confirm your view that you should indeed make all haste to the nearest medical assistance, and advise what you can safely do to help the patient in the meantime.

All parents know that the unexpected crying of a small and as yet none-too-coherent child can sometimes be hard to interpret, but since one cannot always carry quantities of assorted medications on board, a few tips can be useful.

Teething problems

Assuming normal good health (and one would naturally avoid taking small children far out to sea unless fairly certain that they were well, or at least not obviously 'sickening for something'), we found that tooth-cutting posed the most common of early health difficulties. When teething occurs, often presaged as you will know by a hard little cough and eventually accompanied by a pronounced reddening of the cheek, the pain can be considerable. Agonised yells often result. If you do not have the right stuff to smear on the painful gum, so long as your ship has a medicinal bottle of rum (preferably a dark, Demerara type), assistance may lie quite effectively waiting for just this moment in the drinks locker. We are not of course suggesting that a 'slug of the hard stuff' should be used to quieten the baby's howls! It's just that if you dip a finger into a spot of neat rum, then gently and carefully massage the drop into the inflamed gum, it really can provide almost magical relief, and does no harm whatever. The effect is surprisingly long lasting so there is little risk of inducing alcoholism. The advantage of a good-quality dark rum over other spirits is that it is sweet, not too rough, and therefore palatable to a baby.

In addition – a while later, so as not immediately to wash away the effects of the foregoing – something hard and non-toxic to chew on will be a great comfort. Try a nice firm and well-scraped raw carrot.

Later on, when teeth are older, if one is cruising in remote areas where the availability of dentists might be doubtful, it is worth carrying in the ship's medicine chest a little bottle of *Oil of Cloves*, some *Gutta Percha* (in case anyone loses a filling), and a proper *dental mirror* (from good chemists). *Dental Floss*, also available from chemists, can also be a real boon when pain results from something stuck between the teeth, and it is safer in use than fiddling about with tooth-picks or sharp things.

Sunburn

The next most likely trouble, due to the fact that most folk aim to go cruising in high summer, will be the result of over-exposure to sunshine.

Children are especially susceptible, partly because they realise even less readily than adults do that they have 'over-cooked' themselves. And we've all seen adults roast themselves to fiery redness in the first hot sunshine of the season. The real danger with very young European children, however, comes because they often have particularly fair and sensitive skin, easily attacked by the sun's ultra-violet rays. These rays are intensified by reflections off the water, and by the presence of clear, normally relatively unpolluted air, over the sea.

A little exposure to the sun now and again is important to the formation in the body of Vitamin D, but damage to the skin through overdoing it can be excruciatingly painful and actually dangerous. In severe sunburn cases where blistering occurs, risk of infection is high, and scarring may result. So, the greatest care must be taken to see that initial exposure to strong sunlight each year is carefully controlled. A healthy tan should result.

Hands and faces, which usually see a good deal of direct daylight, are of course more resistant than is the rest of our normally covered bodies and limbs, and it may be because hands and faces are what one largely senses with, that the gradual burning of other parts is seldom detected early enough.

So, if a child is allowed to strip off and play in the sunshine of deck or cockpit, or beach, it should on the first day be for not more than fifteen or twenty minutes at the very most, in such an uncovered state. After that time has expired, cover them up with light, natural-fibre clothes, such as a long-sleeved cotton shirt, jeans, and a sun-hat. Certain man-made fibres – nylon, for instance – will not filter out the harmful ultra-violet rays. Next day, sunbathing can be allowed for ten minutes more; say, half an hour in all, and a total of 40–45 minutes on the third day, and so on. Until the tan is thus gradually built up, and pretty well established, longer exposure will make burning a grave possibility for most fair-skinned youngsters – and for adults, too!

One can be fooled by conditions; the sort of hazy sunlight often experienced in fair weather can be just as damaging as more obviously 'hot' sun. But people usually get their worst and most unexpected solar burns on those sparkling, crystal days of brilliant sunshine with a brisk, fresh sailing breeze, for the latter keeps you deceptively cool. A family crew should keep a careful watch on each other's exposed skin, and sing out the moment they notice any reddening at all.

Whether to apply proprietary suntan creams and oils is up to the individual to decide. The kind of cream which contains a definite filter element is in our experience by far the safest. (*Uvistat* do a particularly good one, called *Sun Screen*.)

However, again because of those especially sensitive young skins, it is important to carry out an *allergy check* well in advance, by rubbing a small amount of whatever you intend using onto a bit of the child, such as the inside of a forearm or a tiny area around the shoulder blade, several hours or even days before you attempt to rub oil or cream all over the body and limbs. Anyone who has suffered the appalling agony of being covered in something to which one turns out to be violently allergic will understand the importance of such a test!

And, since someone on board getting sunburnt, even in places, is almost inevitable sooner or later, what best should one apply to the hot and reddened skin, when the damage is irretrievably done? Un-scented cold cream will help to moisturise the area, as well as soothing it (though again apply a small amount as a trial first), but we thought it worth carrying a tube of *Calomine Cream* for this purpose. *Calomine Lotion* is better than nothing, but not nearly so good as the cream, since the drying powder from the lotion can cause severe itching.

Failing any such preparations, make up *a solution of two tablespoons of Bi-carbonate of Soda to half a pint (285ml) of fresh water*, and gently apply that to the stinging places.

The same reflections off the water can cause sore and prickling eyes – in a sense, a sort of ocular sunburn. Cheap children's sunglasses are not really a good idea, partly because their lenses often distort the vision, but mainly because they merely darken the light rays without filtering out those that really do the harm. *Polaroid sunglasses* are much better in this respect, but are expensive things for kids to break, and are very easily scratched. Maybe the best protection where the very young are concerned, is to be gained from a floppy cotton sunhat, which should be secured under the chin – by tape rather than elastic, which is liable to be twanged by other small children on board.

Heat-stroke

This used to be called 'Sunstroke', but it is in fact caused merely by excessive heat, even in shade or indoors, in windless or poorly ventilated conditions. Early symptoms are often the developing of a headache, and a feeling of weakness and dizziness. If nothing is done, the patient's temperature can then start to soar, the skin remaining hot to the touch but bone dry.

Heat-stroke is often brought on by strenuous activity in hot weather, but can simply occur through still air surrounding a hot person. The best way to avoid it – and to counteract its early effects – is to give everyone plenty of water to drink, and either stir into it a pinch of cooking salt, or give them salt tablets to take, if you have some on board. Small folk will be glad to munch plenty of salted snacks such as nuts or potato-crisps, by way of keeping up their salt-intake, and the fact that this will make them thirsty also ensures they'll want to drink plenty too. It's most important that they should.

If the onset of heat-stroke is not noticed in time, and the victim's temperature has started to rise, reduce it as best you can by wiping them all over with cold, wet cloths. The moisture, evaporating on exposed skin, should do the trick. And it won't give them a chill – not in those circumstances!

Where very young children are likely to be troubled with heat-stroke, watch for their becoming fractious, or possibly listless, as first signs. A headache comes next. However, avoidance as always is the best answer in the first place, so in hot weather *make* them drink lots and make sure they get salt somehow. Non-fizzy and un-sweetened drinks are by far the best, and fatty drinks like milk are better avoided; so, unhappily, is ice-cream. If they must have something fizzy, plain soda water is ideal. As to clothes, cool, well-ventilated garments and a sunhat are best at warding off heat-stroke.

Cuts, bruises and burns

Boats being made of so many assorted bits and pieces, cuts and bruises are almost inevitable among the crew, whatever age they are. The skipper can do much to bind sharp things, like split-pins in the rigging, with layers of insulating tape, and can file down potentially dangerous angles and corners wherever they occur on deck or below, but still that unexpected lurch, slip or roll will happen, and someone will sooner or later fall against or grab some unprotected hazard.

In the case of *cuts or grazes*, wash the damaged area very thoroughly with soap (preferably of a non-scented kind) and water, and cover with a sterile dressing, using a bandage or sticky plaster to hold the wad of dressing in place. The modern, skin-like *'Micropore' Surgical Tape* dressings are excellent, allowing the wound to breathe and so heal quickly. Quite a large gash can be successfully held together with this stuff alone, where stitches might in the past have been required.

Bruises should at once be cooled by applying a cloth wrung out repeatedly in cold water. This helps reduce swelling remarkably effectively. Keeping the patient still for half an hour or so will also help the broken internal blood-vessels to clot over and heal up. If the skin is broken, once again wash the area carefully with soap and water before bandaging.

Nipped fingers are best treated in cold water – seawater, which is mildly antiseptic except in harbours, will do very nicely, and if it can't be reached directly by the patient, draw a bucket and dip the nipped part in it, and keep it there. If the water is good and cold, it will hurt considerably, but the damage should be kept in as long as the pain can be borne, because this is far the best way to stop severe swelling.

Burns are again best treated with cold water. Immediately plunge the burnt part into clean seawater or a container of cold drinking water if actual running tapwater is not available. And hold it there until the pain has stopped. The quicker this can be done, the better. Then cover it with a sterile dressing. Avoid smearing burns or scalds with any kind of greasy ointment. Immediate immersion in cold, preferably running water is definitely the best treatment.

Minor cuts, burns, and grazes will heal up very quickly indeed if 'Vitamin E' skin cream is regularly applied for a few days.

Bites and stings

At sea, aggressive insects are not often encountered; it is shore-going which brings this risk. If a bite or sting can be treated within the first few minutes with a liberal application of an *anti-histamine cream*, the stinging or itching will with luck be negligible. Use of anti-histamines later than this, though good, will not be nearly as effective. *Calomine cream* will then help to relieve the discomfort, as will a cold compress.

Try to stop children from vigorously scratching the like of a horse-fly (cleg) or mosquito bite; harsh rubbing like that seems to spread the poison, and merely enlarges the troublesome lump. If they must touch the area at all, get them simply to press hard on the bite with a thumb or finger for a few seconds, then release it. This, by briefly cutting off the surface blood-supply, gives considerable relief and does not irritate the skin.

Jellyfish stings, which in some cases may be very severe indeed, can be effectively treated by giving the victim an anti-histamine tablet at once. *Avomine*, intended primarily as a remedy for travel-sickness (which tends to make the patient a bit drowsy), contains a fair dose of anti-histamine, and does very well indeed for this purpose. Pay attention to the dosage for children on the packet, though, and if the sting is very bad, get medical help.

Artificial respiration

May you never need this, or need to practise it – but should you find yourself having to help someone in this way, *know how to do it*. The easiest and best method of reviving someone whose breathing has stopped, is rather aptly known as *The Kiss of Life*:

1 Lay the victim flat on his back.

Clear away any obstruction in his mouth (he may have swallowed his tongue, or choked on something), then put a folded coat or similar pad under his shoulders.

2 Push his head well back with a hand on his forehead, and pinch his nose shut with finger and thumb.

Hold his mouth open with your other hand.

3 Take a deep breath (dealing with an adult), cover his open mouth completely with yours, and blow to inflate his lungs.

4 Remove your mouth and turn *your* head away while his lungs deflate (he just *might* vomit).

5 Repeat 3 and 4 at your own normal breathing rate until his breathing resumes. When it really has, turn him on his side to let him recover. (Make sure he isn't lying awkwardly on an arm, in this position.)

IMPORTANT: With a small child, you may be able to cover both his mouth and nose with your mouth, easier than doing as above in 3, but remember his lungs are smaller in capacity than yours, so *don't blow too hard or too much* air in. Small puffs will be enough in the case of a really young patient.

"THE KISS OF LIFE"   FIG.10

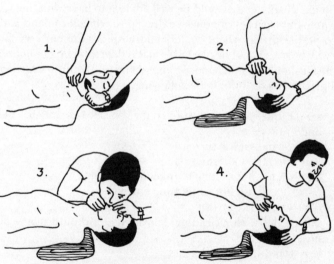

Try practising the 'kiss of life' on your spouse, and on your children, so that you can quickly do the right thing to anyone, in a real emergency.

There are many other possible injuries and ailments, of course, and many books on how to deal with all kinds of medical contingencies. Make a point of carrying such information on board, if you are going to be away from medical assistance for more than a few hours at a stretch. As already mentioned, on quite a number of occasions we found ourselves very glad indeed to have in our boat a copy of the early predecessor to Reader's Digest's *Illustrated Family Medical Encyclopaedia*, despite its considerable bulk, but no doubt there are more compact books which cover what is likely to crop up perfectly adequately.

The one thing that really should be on board any boat, however small, is a *First Aid Kit*.

First aid kits

The sort of boating you are going to indulge in will indicate how simple or elaborate a First Aid box you should carry. Even a racing dinghy crew would be well advised to have with them a water-tight packet of adhesive dressings, while for inland and coastal cruising, where doctors and hospitals are not very far away but might not be reachable in less than three or four hours, the kit should be much more comprehensive. We always carried a plastic box containing the following:

SMALL DRESSINGS AND ADHESIVE PLASTERS (for minor cuts and grazes)
STERILE DRESSINGS (in variety of sizes)
'MICROPORE' SURGICAL TAPE
COTTON BANDAGES (one triangular, as a sling)
CREPE BANDAGE (for supporting hurt joints)
LINT AND COTTONWOOL
COTTONBUDS (for cleaning delicate and awkward places in noses, ears, etc.)
SCISSORS AND TWEEZERS
THERMOMETER
SAFETY PINS
EYE-BATH AND EYE LOTION (or salty water!)
'SAVLON' or other ANTISEPTIC CREAM
LIQUID DISINFECTANT
VITAMIN E CREAM (to aid healing)

OIL OF CLOVES
GUTTA PERCHA
DENTAL FLOSS
DENTAL MIRROR
Miniature bottle of DEMERARA RUM
VASELINE
ANTI-HISTAMINE CREAM
CALOMINE CREAM
SUN-FILTERING CREAM
AVOMINE TABLETS (for jellyfish stings or seasickness)
MARZINE OR STUGERON TABLETS (for seasickness)
MOGADON TABLETS (for tense and sleepless skippers)
MILK OF MAGNESIA TABLETS (for indigestion)
CALIFORNIA SYRUP OF FIGS (for constipation)
INSECT REPELLENT (for obvious reasons)
SOLUBLE ASPIRIN TABLETS
REALLY POWERFUL PAIN-KILLER TABLETS – seek medical advice on these, they're in case of really severe injury only, or other acutely intense pain such as renal colic – and NOT for kids!

The important thing with any First Aid Kit, be it a ready-equipped pack from a yacht chandler or chemist, or one you have made up for yourself, is to *keep it fully stocked*. When you notice that a supply of items such as aspirin, seasick pills, or small sticking plasters, is almost used up, be sure to put it on the shopping list there and then, or in accordance with the natural perversity of inanimate things, there won't be any left when you most need them.

Obviously if someone on board has had some proper First Aid Training before setting out, the whole crew will be that much better off if and when any physical damage or illness, however minor, occurs. It can be very hard to concentrate on reading how to deal with a sudden and possibly frightening situation when the patient is lying there in trouble right in front of you and begging you to *do* something. It therefore seems extremely sensible for both skipper and mate to spend a few winter evenings attending classes in First Aid, just in case . . .

Children's diseases

It is for your doctor, not us, to suggest or apply treatment when a youngster gets Chicken Pox, Whooping Cough, or whatever of the usual 'childish' ailments is currently doing the rounds. On several occasions, however, we had a daughter unexpectedly go down with one of the various things of this sort, just before we were due to go cruising on our annual holiday. However, once the initial stages of the illness and any 'crisis peak' associated with it are over, children will mostly benefit from a good dose of sea air and some gentle but healthy exercise.

The only problem, then, is that of quarantine.

To be absolutely correct, you can look up the Admiralty Code of Signals, and fly the appropriate flags in your rigging, to indicate to others (who are able to read said signal) that you have 'plague' on board. We're not even telling you what the correct flags are though, for the simple reason that if you do fly them, as we once did, you will have visitor after visitor coming alongside to ask what they mean – which is just the opposite effect of what you intended in the circumstances!

If you do take a quarantined family cruising, it goes without saying that you are under obligation not to take the infectious persons ashore or onto other yachts where they might pass on the infection. But it is still possible to find uncrowded beaches or isolated anchorages, away from shore-side temptations in most cruising areas, and places where one can go for walks, or explore creeks in the dinghy, or do other things that don't involve rubbing shoulders with strangers. So with adequate forethought and care, a really good, if possibly rather different family cruise can still be enjoyed.

'Tummy bugs'

Travelling away from home *anywhere*, one is liable to pick up strange bacteria in food or water from sources other than those to which one's digestive system is used, merely because one doesn't have the right antibodies. Sickness and diarrhoea may result (internal efforts to remove the offenders). One can obtain medicines to help, so ask the doctor if carrying a supply of maybe *Guanimycil*, or perhaps *Lomotil* (tablets) might be a good idea for your family in such circumstances. Like a lot of things in life, 'a little of what you fancy' may do you good – but take care not to overdo the dosage, particularly where children are involved! It may often be best to take the advice of an old Scottish doctor who tended our family through several such bouts of tummy infections: 'Take nothing whatever – no food, no drink, and above all, no broth – for the first four to five hours. Then take a few sips of water. If that stays down, after a further hour try a cup of weak tea with a plain biscuit or some *lightly* buttered "fingers" of toast.'

The same good man had further advice if perchance after six hours not even plain water would stay down – as sometimes can happen. 'Mix 1 part of Scotch whisky (nothing else will do) with 15 parts of water – no stronger and no weaker – and even if in the ordinary way you simply can't bear to drink or even smell whisky, like that it really will stay down.' And it does!

Constipation

This is a common complaint during the first few days of living on board a boat. Often it is due simply to a change of diet, a change of routine, or merely the change of surroundings, but it is surprising how many people, adults as well as children, bring it upon themselves, just by being shy about visiting the ship's toilet. Because in many small craft this is merely curtained off or in rather a noticeable part of the accommodation, some folk seem frightened and bashful about 'going in there' (and making involuntary noises or smells) when other members of the crew are down below decks. It's almost as though they thought they were the only person in the world who (embarrassingly) found the necessity to vacate their waste body products every day. Thus, instead of 'going' when they normally do, the time their body is used to passes, and with it the immediate urge.

When engaged in skippered charter work, we were surprised at the number of people (particularly females and young boys) who went to all sorts of lengths to persuade everyone else up on deck before they would dare to enter the doorway of and enclose themselves in the toilet compartment. Even then, constipation proved a frustrating and uncomfortable condition for quite a few, until they rather pitifully asked for a laxative.

California Syrup of Figs is an old, but mild and very effective remedy for young and old alike, which we always had on board. *Milk of Magnesia* (in sufficient quantity) has similar effect. But there are other things one can do, like providing a good diet with lots of wholemeal bread and bran for 'roughage'.

We also found that having, pinned on the door or bulkhead opposite where one sat 'enthroned' on the loo, a selection of written instructions, such as how to use the liferaft, and don lifejackets, or light emergency flares, helped to distract the mind from any difficulties, and while one is reading the body relaxes, and can operate its peristaltic action in its own good time. This reading material had a second advantage, displayed where it was. After a few days, everyone on board who could read, knew by heart how to secure and launch the liferaft, in case they ever had to!

Coping with seasickness

Lucky the family who does not have at least one member prone to seasickness! The chances are, however, that although tiny babies, used as they have recently been to surviving motion in the warm and watery womb as their mothers moved about, are at first seldom given to travel sickness, this immunity is usually lost completely by the age of one year. After that, quite a number of kids fall victim to travel sickness in one form or another, and although in time their susceptibility will lessen (usually around the age of puberty), they may be put off the idea of boating being a 'fun thing', unless something can be done to make life in a seaway easier for them.

Fortunately there are a number of things which help a great deal – and may, with a bit of luck, even totally prevent seasickness in the first place.

As with any medicine, it would be wrong simply to mete out a dose of 'sick pills' to a child (or a 'first time' adult) unless you *know* for a fact that they really will otherwise feel or be seasick. So until a child has actually proved that it does get sick when a boat starts lurching or rolling, it is unfair to feed it with a drug 'just in case'. Two of our three girls tended to be seasick almost with certainty, at least for the first few days of a cruise; the other didn't.

Keep nibbling

We found that apart from wave action, lack of food was the worst culprit, and it has long been known that a frequent input of non-fatty foods is an excellent way of preventing the onset of travel sickness. For this reason, we tried always to have a normal (but carefully selected) meal beforehand, which we aimed to finish some forty minutes before getting under way. This gave time for digestion to start its work adequately, without the next bout of peckishness having a chance to set in.

Unfortunately human stomachs seem to have only two real senses: 'Full', and 'Empty'. And the one reading 'Empty' is virtually identical to that which, one realises often too late, really meant 'Sick'. So, if you keep stoking it in a modest sort of way, it will not get the chance to register 'Empty' at all, and your brain may never think of sickness.

About half an hour or so after departure, biscuits (*not* chocolate ones) can therefore be handed round to great advantage, and some more nibbles, such as dried fruit, will probably be welcome from time to time throughout the day, between meals: a very little snack at regular intervals. The sort of fruit bars one can buy in most Health Food shops are ideal for these occasions – very tasty and energy-giving, without being over-sweet. In suitably small quantities, snacks of this kind do not interfere with one's personal 'internal clock'.

And when it is lunch or supper time, a reasonably substantial meal of some kind should always be produced, if at all possible; the body has come to expect it, and must be forgiven for rebelling if nothing turns up. Some yachts, such as multihulls, are much easier to cook in at sea than others, but if going below and working over a stove is likely to make the cook ill, a better idea on open-sea crossings and even on long coastal hops, might be to prepare things before departure, using carefully stowed vacuum flasks of soup, stew, and of course hot water for making warm drinks.

Seasick kids

One has to remember that children can vomit with much less difficulty than most adults, and though the very first time at sea may come as a most unpleasant surprise to them (as to everyone else), and may even be a rather frightening experience if they haven't endured it before, it is likely to be quickly forgotten by them (if not by whoever had to clear up), *so long as not too much fuss is made.*

Except in the highly unlikely event of it becoming a pretty continuous state throughout a passage, with no signs of recovery between bouts, there is absolutely no need to worry. So long as the parents can treat the first few occasions in a fairly matter-of-fact way, being gently sympathetic without 'laying it on', the child itself will make little of it.

Our most frequent victim, Eileen, maintained that *she* didn't mind in the least; this was hard for us to believe, of course, but she has always been quite adamant about it – which was a considerable relief to her father, who as skipper of the vessel that inflicted the condition on her as a result of his decision to carry on sailing in rough seas, naturally felt terrible about being the cause of her 'suffering'.

'Sick pills'

No rule of thumb here; the correct and most effective pill is likely to depend on the individual concerned. Most proprietary brands contain some kind of sedative, and many use anti-histamine. *Avomine*, whose active ingredient is Promethazine Theoclate, is an example of this kind, which makes it suitable (see p. 92) as a medicine to counteract the effects of severe jellyfish stings, as well as working in the accepted sense. It makes many people quite drowsy, though, and while this may not be a bad thing where children are affected, on a long, rough crossing for instance, in that they can safely be tucked up in their bunks, the very young must have only a small portion of one of the tiny tablets, which should not be repeated for at least eight hours. An overdose results in very heavy drugging indeed.

We found that *Marzine* (containing Cyclizine) was less soporific than *Avomine*, and worked well without obvious side-effects of any kind for two of our number (including the skipper), but again one had to be careful to give the very young only a small part of one of the minute tablets, and not to repeat the dose for a good eight hours.

Nowadays, the newer drug *Stugeron* (Cinnarzine) which was more or less developed by yachtsmen for yachtsmen, has been very well tested, and if taken according to the instructions, can really make all the difference – even for readily seasick adults as well as for children – between a miserable passage and a fully enjoyable trip, whether on deck or down in the cabin, despite heavy weather.

DO BE CAREFUL WITH ANY OF THESE DRUGS. Some people turn out to be wildly allergic to some of the ingredients, even in the simpler pills such as *Sealegs* (Meclozine Hydrochloride) or *Kwells* (Hyoscine Hydrobromide), never mind the more powerful ones already named. We suggest a good scheme is to have a few trials at home, perhaps when motoring, so that if an allergic rash or other unpleasant reaction crops up, medical help will not be hard to find. Such cases are very rare indeed, fortunately.

Keep warm – and keep interested

Inactivity, strangely, is just as bad as over-activity, when it comes to making you feel seasick. The crew who sits huddled in a corner of the cockpit, hanging on with white knuckles as the yacht bucks and lurches, is as well on the way to succumbing as the crew who has just performed some extra-strenuous struggle on deck, changing jibs or reefing, in the same conditions.

If someone starts getting a bit broody-looking, and yawning

widely, and they are at all capable of holding the boat on course for even a few minutes at a time, set them at once to steering; the concentration they will have to devote to helming may well save them from getting worse. If they cannot steer, try getting a few word games going, such as 'Twenty Questions', or singing songs. It's often just a matter of distracting the mind from thinking the wrong thoughts!

One of the worst promoters of seasickness, however, is cold. If you once get badly chilled at sea, it can be all too hard to get warm again, partly because of a possible fear that going below decks out of the wind might make one ill. In trying to adjust its own inner temperature control, the body burns much energy, and to do this it needs food – the thought of which might already be repulsive. A particularly nasty 'vicious circle'! So, when on passage, make sure everyone who comes on deck is warmly dressed and windproofed as much as possible if the weather's at all grey.

Oilskins should for this reason be on the big side, so as to allow room underneath for several sweaters and maybe a second pair of trousers. A woolly hat can be a surprising help, even in summer; it's amazing how much heat we lose out of the top of our heads!

If garments are tight, inactivity is to a certain extent forced on the wearer, and sitting still is one of the quickest ways of getting cold (no matter how much you're wearing).

Natural fibre clothing (wool or cotton) are generally far better at keeping one warm at sea than synthetics, in that they absorb sweat and let your skin breathe. However for real cosiness, modern 'polar suits', even with their 'fake' fleecy linings, are excellent, and to our way of thinking, *very* well worth the expense if one does much cruising in a cold climate.

At night

Particularly at night, make sure the whole crew is kept warmly covered, whether they are on deck or below, for the body naturally tends to lower its own temperature levels at the time when it is used to going to sleep, whether it actually does sleep or not. Most ocean-going yachtsmen find it takes two or three days of regular watch-keeping before their personal time-clocks adjust to night watches, so the family that does maybe only one or two overnight passages in a season may well find keeping warm at the helm in the 'wee small hours' before dawn, extremely difficult.

Here again, plenty of handy snacks of a non-fatty nature, and occasional mugs of something hot to drink will make a world of difference, and the prospect of daylight and breakfast can be regarded with happy anticipation, rather than longed for with a wild and wretched desperation!

Fatigue – the real danger

Above all risks at sea, excessive tiredness is probably the most dangerous condition to get into. You can take your gales, freak seas, shoals, fogs, and potential collision situations, and with a bit of normal knowledge, commonsense, and ordinary seamanlike skills, the chances are you'll cope far more easily and satisfactorily than you at first thought you might . . . *unless you are badly tired*.

Fatigue, and its development, physical exhaustion, are the real evils at sea, because in trying to keep the body functioning through a tired state, the mind rapidly loses the capability of making the right decisions quickly.

If your brain tends to err on the safe side when it is weary (and how do you know it really will?), you are perhaps safer as a skipper or helmsman than the person who optimistically makes himself think 'It'll be all right . . .', and just carries on. It's all too easy to sit there hoping that the situation will improve on its own, without anyone having to act. If we are honest with ourselves, that is precisely the state of mind which most of us who go to sea *will* experience at some time or other.

Crews stand a better chance than skippers to snatch a little proper sleep, though it may be in odd moments or off-watch below decks, restoring their energy in mind and body before the next watch or burst of activity catches up with them.

Skippers don't rest so easily

Especially when his young children are on board, the skipper of a family yacht, unless he is unusually self-controlled and placid, or just not the worrying kind, may well find difficulty in sleeping when the boat is on passage. However good his wife or other members of his crew may be at steering, navigating, and handling the ship, sails, and engine, he may feel very deeply the sense of over-all responsibility which indeed is his, and his alone.

Sleep is quite likely to elude such a person. For a start many skippers spend most of their sailing time on deck, or for a few minutes at a time engrossed at the chart-table before dashing back to the cockpit to settle the boat on a new course. It is only when a skipper gets his head down in a bunk that all the peculiar noises of the yacht making her way over the seas will come to him, as it were for the first time. There may be clonks, and clinks, or weird tappings and creaks. And that odd sound of trickling water, seemingly somewhere down in the bilges . . .

The anxious and tired mind may well have difficulty in accepting these sounds either as natural, to convince him that there really is nothing at all wrong and no leaks and no imminent rigging or rudder failures, or in accepting the sheer volume of sound and shutting it out. The row can seem quite deafening, yet all he wants is a bit of peace and quiet and untroubled slumber. So the poor chap lies awake, eyes defiantly shut, but his brain racing, bothering about one thing after another.

Back on deck in time for the next watch, he is now by no means refreshed, and if weather conditions deteriorate, he will become even more fatigued – and more likely to make the wrong decision in a sudden moment of crisis, or even when it comes to making port and berthing the boat.

And when the passage is over? Why, the kids wake up and want to play about and have breakfast and talk and shout, and as sure as anything either there is some reason why they can't be taken ashore, or if they can, the ship is perhaps not lying in an easy berth, and Father is again going to be denied the chance to sleep really deeply or refreshingly. 'You lot go ashore,' he says stoically. 'I'll keep an eye on the ship.'

And they do, and he does – and therefore does no more than doze lightly, what with keeping an ear out for approaching craft or feet on deck, or the scraping noise and gentle jerk denoting a dragging anchor. Deep, relaxed sleep may by now prove right out of the question for him. This is where his wife and Mate must take a firm hand, and if necessary literally 'baby-sit' for her husband on her return from shopping, keeping the kids quiet somehow, and *making* the skipper have a proper sleep.

As a family, we have always been firmly against the taking of any kind of drug for any but the most valid reasons; but when a vessel's skipper becomes exhausted, whether he is in charge of a supertanker or a 2-ton yacht, both his ship and his crew are put at risk. So in these circumstances, a mild but effective sleeping pill, such as *Mogadon* can be of very great benefit – not just to the man or woman who needs it, but in their subsequent more normal and balanced attitude to the rest of the crew, the handling of the boat, and the world in general. The advantage of this particular preparation is that *should* an important situation arise, one can quite easily 'wake through' the drug, and can act mentally and physically without any restraint or 'wuzziness'. In other words, one can 'over-ride' the relaxing effects without difficulty – and incidentally, go readily back to sleep afterwards, when the trouble is over.

Like any other sleeping pill, however, one requires a doctor's prescription to get it, so it pays to explain exactly why you require it, and the reasons why you do *not* want a 'knockout' drug. And naturally you will keep the bottle where the children will never find it – not that *Mogadon* is actually very dangerous: an overdose thereof is not usually fatal.

The important thing to remember is that the family skipper – and the family mate, who as Mother and Cook has probably a far greater share of the work on board when the children are small – *both need their sleep*. In fact, the closer the rhythm of shipboard life adheres to the normal rhythm of home life, the better chance that the holiday will remain the happy, cheerful event to which everyone can look forward keenly, each year.

Shifting the adults' day forward a couple of hours to fit in with the children's things, as suggested on p. 83, is something one gets completely used to after two or three days; but do try to stick to regular mealtimes, whether at sea or in port.

Maintaining your vitality

Maybe because of consuming certain processed foods and drinks, or for other reasons, many people find themselves running out of steam towards late afternoon or evening, when on a cruise. The onset of fading light may then seem more depressing than it should, and your 'worrying' type of skipper, or over-taxed Mother, may find themselves getting far less fun and pleasure than they should from their boating holiday. All this really may be nothing more than the result of a vitamin deficiency – not because you are not getting the usual amount of vitamins, so much as because you may be burning them up far too rapidly.

If you or your crew do experience this sort of feeling, try supplementing your diet with *Vitamin B* in the form of *Brewer's Yeast Tablets*, available from most chemists. (Yes, we know there is Vitamin B in beer, but increasing your beer intake makes you use Vitamin B far quicker! Alas, this is *not* the answer!) You may find that a single dose of say three tablets at breakfast, or a few more later in the day as required, can have the most astonishingly buoyant effect.

Yeast is not a medicine or a chemical, it's a food in its own right, and it cannot do you any harm. (If you take too much, your body just 'passes' what it doesn't require.) Anyway, if you are like us, you may find a daily supplement of yeast, however small a dose you take, will have an appreciable effect on your capacity to enjoy life, especially when the weather is rotten and the wind's getting up yet again, and you have been having one of those mercifully rare but none-the-less horrible 'sell the boat' days, when everything seems to be going wrong. But don't sell the boat; try swallowing a few yeast tablets instead. You may find things looking a good deal better, within the next twenty minutes or so . . .

6
Food and Water

The various snack-foods, which are so invaluable for short boat-trips and on passage, have already been mentioned, but if the family is going to spend a fortnight or more on board, every effort should be made to provide the crew with plenty of fresh produce, as well as tinned or packaged foods – assuming one does not expect to be fed ashore every day.

There is, of course, no harm in keeping a stock of good-quality 'convenience foods' which save work for the ship's cook, and give her (or him) a break too.

The main trouble with most packaged foods is, first, that they are usually something of an 'additive cocktail', with lots of 'flavour enhancer', such as monosodium glutamate, as well as other chemical ingredients, and therefore must really be interspersed with proper fresh-food meals or snacks, to ensure a healthy over-all intake. Secondly, the dried or packaged meals require a considerable amount of additional water for cooking purposes, so the yacht's tanks will have to be large enough to cope. If there are infants or toddlers on board, water consumption will anyway be very high.

'Water, water . . .'

When our kids were very small, we found we were using water during a family cruise at the rate of approximately twice the amount per day we required *for the same people* ten years later! (See Chapter 3, pp. 56–7.) In those early days, however, the water capacity in our little catamaran was not very great, so we took to using tinned, rather than dehydrated convenience foods, as the canned stuff often contained all or most of its own fluid requirement for the cooking.

On the subject of water, its storage over a period can create problems, as most people know. It behoves one to taste and check in a glass the appearance of any water before it is blindly piped into the ship's tanks, and even then it is well worth putting a purifying tablet in with it. If you can't get such tablets, you can prevent the formation of bacterial growths and nasty taste in the water tank by putting in a small quantity of ordinary *bi-carbonate of soda*, about one level tablespoon for every 10 gallons (45–50 litres).

When young children need extra water, a number of one- or two-gallon containers can be carried, and again, about *a saltspoonful (the tip of a teaspoon, say) of bi-carbonate per gallon* will keep the contents in good order. (No, it doesn't make the water fizzy, or taste odd – nor does it do the digestion any harm, needless to say!)

Fresh bread

If you require bread to keep, the British style of Sliced Pan Loaf will keep moist and soft in its plastic wrapper for up to a week. Unfortunately brown bread of the nice 'roughage' sort, even though packed the same way, does not keep quite so well (about five days, pleasantly, in a cool locker) because of being a drier mix to start with, but both are much better at keeping than bread baked, however deliciously, the French way. (It's seldom moist after about 24 hours.)

Oatcakes, water-biscuits, and the whole range of rye or wheaten crispbreads, such as the *Ryvita* and *Ry-King*, keep crisp for ages if stored in an airtight container, but aren't a bit like the spongy texture of the 'real thing'.

We always thought it worth while to carry a bag or two of flour and the ingredients for making a few nice hot drop-scones and Irish soda bread (see recipes on pp. 115–17), to be able to give everyone a treat once in a while, for instance when cooped up by bad weather. These are very easy to make, using the simple sort of galley equipment found in most small cruising craft.

If you have no oven on board, visit your local camping shop, and see if you can get one of the various little camping ovens on the market, some of which fold away completely flat. We for many years used one called a *'Cubex' Wonder Oven*, consisting of a galvanised metal box complete with door and wire shelf, and a bottom specially adapted to fit over and benefit efficiently from the top of the ordinary gas or Primus stove. It worked extremely well, and when off-duty, was used as an extra stowage locker, lashed into a corner in the galley. However, for drop-scones anyway, you don't need an oven, and the same applies to soda bread, as the recipes will show.

Of special value on a cruise where exercise and fresh air promote a healthy appetite, is a good supply of cakes and interesting biscuits: fruitcake, gingerbread, and banana-bread (see p. 117) all keep moist and fresh for long periods, so can be made in advance, and produced at strategic moments.

Having a few secret surprises hidden at the back of a locker somewhere (so long as you don't forget them) is a good idea; an occasional luxury item which nobody knew about, produced unexpectedly, will help to make any cook popular and any cruise the more memorable. We'll always remember the bitterly cold, wet and windy summer cruise some years ago, when our flagging spirits were suddenly lifted by the opening of a large, sealed tin which had been concealed at the back of the cook's private locker. It contained a fully iced, well laced, and correctly decorated Christmas cake. It couldn't have been more appropriate!

A pre-cruise bake-up

Before leaving home, make a supply of favourite goodies, such as cereal 'fingers' or other munchy things. We found it a good idea to keep certain varieties just for boating, without ever producing them at home in the ordinary way, so that they were yet another of the aspects of going afloat that our young crew would come to look forward to. Using an air-tight box, choice things of this nature will keep well.

And so will 'soft' margarine, in its plastic tub, so long as the lid is on properly, and it is in a cool locker. Some brands are remarkably like butter to taste, but have the great advantage of remaining spreadable however cold or hot the weather becomes, whereas real butter gets almost brittle after a chilly night on board, and turns into liquid in a heatwave.

Keeping up the vitamins

Fresh fruit and vegetables are of course the finest source of vitamins, and should be stored in an airy locker if possible. Unless you can't live without them, it is better not to try keeping fresh onions in a small boat; they stink the place out in no time and make *everyone's* eyes water if the cook starts peeling them below decks. Dried onions are really just as good for most purposes.

If the cruise is for longer than about two weeks, dishing out a few extra vitamin pills at breakfast each day will pay dividends. *Vitamin C* tablets will considerably reduce the chances of picking up strange infections ashore, and *Vitamin B* in the form of Yeast Tablets (see p. 106) should keep everyone cheerful even in depressing conditions.

To supplement your crew's diet further with the goodness of other vitamins, try offering raw carrots around. Grated on a salad they are sweet and juicy, but scraped clean and nibbled as a snack, they can become extremely popular with all age-groups, the more so if the carrots are not too large.

Salad dishes of any kind should form a good part of the week's menu, but can't be kept fresh for long, apart from carrots, tomato, cucumber, and the like. Buy lettuce just before departure if you can, and bring it on board already washed, in a plastic tub or polybag. Or, of course, wash it in *clean* seawater.

We used to grow a pack of cress on the galley worktop, or wedged near a cabin window or the hatch; that's a grand source of vitamins, and adds flavour to salad and savoury sandwiches.

Alfalfa seeds (from Health Food shops), sprouted on board in a jar placed on its side with muslin held on by an elastic band in place of the lid, are absolutely packed with vitamins; the seeds should be wetted twice daily, and the water poured out again through the muslin. They very quickly grow into a tangle of sprouts and softened seeds, and you eat the lot, sprinkled on salads, or 'bread-and-spreads' of one kind or another. Salads are a good idea from the cook's point of view, being quick and easy to prepare.

Keep it simple

As it's supposed to be Mother's holiday too, make a Ship's Law to the effect that the cook is never allowed (note that last word) to wash up. (Well, *hardly* ever.) Then naturally, so as to reduce the washing-up for the rest of the crew, encourage her to prepare quick, easy meals most of the time, in return for this kindness!

Packet mashed-potatoes, rice, spaghetti and macaroni, are quicker to do – and use less gas – than 'live' potatoes. But do be careful never to spill rice grains into the bilges: we did, and kept finding them for years afterwards. (Don't spill pickled beetroot, either.)

Minced meat is economical, and versatile. It too cooks rapidly, saving fuel as well as time. Other meats are more messy; chops muck up the grill, and so do sausages, unless they are fried – and too much fried food is to be avoided, especially if a rough passage is in the offing. Fried egg is the worst of the lot in this respect!

Fresh salad, instead of cooked vegetables, make a simple and highly nutritious accompaniment to any meat or fish dish – and won't steam up the galley the way boiling vegetables will. Talking of steaming; with the right kind of pan combination, vegetables can easily be cooked over a pan of boiling rice, potatoes, or pasta.

After the main course has been demolished, fresh fruit, tubs of yoghurt, slices of cake, etc., will avoid the need for a cooked pudding. Besides requiring no preparation, they contain less sugar than most tinned desserts, and being fresh (or nearly so) are that much better for you anyway.

Pressure-pot cookery

When it comes to cooking in a small boat, a good-quality pressure-cooker can be very useful. Some people are frightened by the things at first, but if you follow the instructions bravely, there is nothing to fear; they have safety valves and are perfectly safe even should the relief valve stick – and it won't if you keep it clean. The thing is to practise with it, until you get used to it. And then you'll use it for everything you can think of!

The big advantages of a pressure-cooker on board are that it saves time spent in the galley, saves fuel, and won't spill even if knocked over, so the safety aspect is a particular boon. It also keeps cooking smells to a minimum, which in a confined space is worth consideration. Using a clockwork timer to tell you when the meal is cooked, you can go out on deck and enjoy the sailing while it's down there doing the work for you. But what we like most is the flavour of food cooked this way. Just as the advertisements say, all the goodness stays in, and the rapid cooking times mean that fewer vitamins are destroyed in the process than is the case with an ordinary saucepan.

Instant foods

'Instant' soups, 'Pot Noodles' and the like, which need only boiling water added, are a great help during cold passages. In a wildly lurching galley, though, get yourself well wedged or strapped into a secure corner before trying to pour water from one receptacle into another. Lift *both* things, e.g. both the kettle *and* the mug – and don't do it over bare legs. It is far easier to pour things accurately this way in bouncy conditions than trying to slosh the right amount of water, soup, etc., into a mug wedged maybe in the sink, where the arm holding the pan or kettle is inevitably going to be moving in a different manner to what is fixed to the ship. If you lift both items, both move together.

As we have said, we would not recommend living on instant foods for days at a time. Fresh food is generally healthier in the long run.

Products such as *Coffee-mate*, *U.H.T.* or *Longlife* milk and cream, or your favourite brand of powdered milk (and do experiment; some are very like the real thing, especially if allowed to 'stand' in a jug overnight before use, after mixing) are one of the blessings of modern holiday boating. Gone at last are what used in latter days to be a seemingly endless succession of dreary hunts for milk.

Stoking the baby

One can of course load up with large supplies of the various little pots of baby food, but assuming your infant is being or has been weaned, here is one member of the crew who needs plenty of vitamins and fresh food.

The answer is to buy the ship a manually operated purée maker, such as the *Mouli-Baby*, which looks like a little saucepan with a finely perforated base, above which clips a metal paddle-blade worked by a rotating handle. The softer parts of practically any cooked food other than some meat can be forced through the holes, making a nourishing paste which may be spoon-fed while still warm. The device is easily cleaned and very tough.

We 'Mouli-ed' almost everything that the adults were having, and it all went down a treat – with the memorable exception of curry. (A mushed-up raw banana soothed the resulting tingling instantly, in case you are wondering.)

Give them a treat, when gale-bound

It can be very depressing if bad weather keeps you cooped up in harbour, particularly if it's raining. Even the usual on-board games seem not quite so much fun. So this is when the cook and mother can boost the morale of her crew by pulling out a few stops. It's marvellous the effect that even a simple culinary treat can have, and the feeling of togetherness it generates as you sit there enjoying a special feast is worth a little effort.

This happened one time when we were stormbound in Mallaig, away out on the far western coast of Scotland. Cold northern rain had been sheeting down all day, swirling round into any opening at every gust, and dirt, muck and seagull droppings had been blowing down onto our decks from the quays above since the previous evening.

Oilskinned, booted, and battling against the wind, with the smaller ones holding on tight, we had spent the early afternoon doing a bit of shopping, and after our return the mate had settled into her galley. The 'breath of air' had put new life into the rest of us, and after a vicious game of 'Snakes-and-Ladders', the prevailing Arthur Ransome (*We Didn't Mean To Go To Sea*) was read aloud to the accompanying shrilling of the gale in our rigging, the sploshes of squall-driven wavelets along our fibreglass hull sides, and an increasingly interesting aroma from the direction of the little cooker.

Eventually, an unusual amount of cutlery, together with some very 'polite' items such as proper side-plates and extra teaspoons, was handed up, and reading came to an abrupt halt just after the bit where Sinbad the kitten had been rescued from his drifting crate in the North Sea, while we all laid the table.

A full, four-course dinner ensued, starting with fresh melon, all prettily cut and topped with glacé cherries, followed by roast chicken, roast potatoes, bread sauce and gravy, peas (ex-frozen), celery hearts (ex-tinned), and a glass or two of white wine, very well watered for the young ones. The sweet was a special favourite, once introduced by a visiting crew: tinned pears with diced gingerbread soaked in the syrup, topped with custard and a blob of fresh cream from the local dairy. Cheese (also local) and biscuits came next, and coffee was accompanied by a mint chocolate. Or two.

It had taken a considerable amount of juggling with various containers, all of which had had to take turns on the two burners and in and out of the tiny oven, but the result was good enough to be hugely enjoyed.

Teatime on other such stormbound occasions might be

enlivened with a special baking of fresh drop-scones cooked in the bottom of the big frying-pan in place of the traditional griddle. These would be served straight from the pan, to be 'buttered' and eaten hot at once.

Irish soda bread – often from a somewhat adapted recipe (see p. 116) was another favourite, particularly when it could be eaten still warm, and exceptionally good with bramble or blackcurrant jelly.

Recipes for success with your crew:

This is not a cookery book, but one or two tried and tested recipes for treats which prove popular on family cruises may be thought useful.

DROP-SCONES *(Scotch Pancakes)*
½ lb (225 g, or just over ¾ pint) self-raising flour
(If using plain flour, add ½ tsp bi-carbonate
of soda and 1 tsp cream of tartar.)
A pinch of salt
A pinch of sugar, if you like
½ pint (250 ml) milk
3–4 eggs

Mix all dry ingredients together in a bowl, then make a well in the centre and beat in the eggs and half of the milk, until a thick, creamy batter is formed. (Use a rotary beater, or hard work with a fork, to achieve this.) Stir in the remaining milk.

Heat a lightly greased griddle (girdle) or frying-pan, and drop dessertspoonfuls of the mixture onto it, reasonably spaced out. Drop it from the end, rather than the side of the spoon, to produce round scones instead of strange-looking ones. When bubbles appear, turn them over with a spatula, and cook until lightly browned on both sides.

By this time the aroma will have got the crew all ready and waiting. Serve the first batch at once, so that they can be buttered and eaten still hot. But do eat your own in the galley, or you'll miss out completely!

Drop-scones are a high-protein food (eggs and milk). Just the thing after a hard sail!

SODA BREAD

Popular in Ireland, soda bread tastes just as delectable in other countries too. It can be baked in a loaf tin in the oven, or made (the traditional way) into a flat cake marked out in quarters, properly called 'farls'.

Soda farls can be cooked on a baking sheet in the oven, or on a griddle or in the bottom of a *heavy-based* frying-pan over a burner.

Soda bread can either be white, brown, or even wholemeal, depending on the flour used. Ordinary self-raising flour is not ideal, as it is milled from a soft type of wheat, whereas plain flour is usually produced from harder wheats. In some places, one can actually buy proper 'soda bread self-raising flour', which is of course perfect for the job.

Soda bread is traditionally made with sour milk or buttermilk. Not many yachts carry cans of buttermilk, but sour milk does occur by accident now and then. Failing that, fresh milk can easily be 'soured' in a few moments, by stirring in a few drops of lemon juice. If you have no milk, you can still make excellent soda bread just using water!

You need:

> 1 lb (450 g, or just over 1¼ pints) plain flour
> 1 tsp salt
> ½ tsp bi-carbonate of soda
> ½ tsp cream of tartar (but if using water instead of milk, double that)
> Almost ½ pint (roughly 275 ml) sour milk or water, to mix.

Mix all dry ingredients together well, then using a metal spoon, quickly and lightly stir in just enough liquid to give a soft dough – not a sticky one. (If it is, add a little more flour.)

Turn the dough out onto a floured surface and either shape it into a long cake to fit a loaf tin, or fashion it into a disc about ½ inch (1.25 cm) thick, and cut into farls (quarters). Do not separate the pieces.

Bake a soda loaf in a hot oven for approximately thirty minutes. To be sure it is done, turn the loaf out and tap the bottom of it. If it sounds hollow, it is ready. Exact cooking time will depend on the oven, as well as the shape of the loaf.

If making farls, they should be put onto a pre-heated, lightly greased griddle, or onto the base of a thick-bottomed frying-pan, and cooked over a burner at a medium setting. In only 5–7 minutes the first side should become nicely browned, so turn it over and complete cooking the other side.

Best eaten slightly warm.

Goodies to make in advance

Three examples of the sort of thing that a day's baking at home, can provide in the way of special 'boat treats' for the family:

LISA'S BANANA-BREAD

1 lb (450 g) plain flour
½ lb (225 g) butter
4 eggs, well beaten
14 oz (400 g) sugar
2 tsp bi-carbonate of soda
2 tsp lemon juice
1 tsp salt
3 tabs sour cream, or buttermilk, or sour(ed) milk
6 bananas, well mashed

Prepare the oven at 350°F, Gas Mark 4, and line both a 1 lb and a 2 lb loaf tin with greased, greaseproof paper.

Rub the butter into the flour. When it resembles fine breadcrumbs, stir in all the other dry ingredients (not the bananas).

Beat in first the eggs, then the lemon juice and cream (milk, or buttermilk), and finally the banana mush.

Pour the mixture into the tins and bake for about one hour. Test with a skewer. If it comes out clean, the loaf is ready.

When thoroughly cool, wrap in foil. It will keep a long time until opened, when it will vanish rather rapidly!

BISCUIT-CRUMB CAKE
2 oz (about 50 g) butter or hard margarine
2 tabs golden syrup
4½ oz (125 g) cooking chocolate
½ lb (225 g) plain sweet biscuits

The type of biscuits used naturally alters the flavour of the end product with this one. We found digestive biscuits particularly nice.

Crumb the biscuits fairly finely by putting them into a polythene bag and crushing them with a rolling-pin.

Melt the margarine, golden syrup and chocolate in a large saucepan, and stir in the biscuit crumbs. Mix to a smooth paste.

Invert a baking sheet, and oil the bottom. Oil a flan ring, and place it on the oiled baking sheet, then press the mixture down firmly into the ring, smoothing off the top.

Leave to cool, then remove the flan ring and wrap the cake in kitchen foil. It keeps like that for several months.

'GUDGE'
½ lb (225 g) golden syrup. (Put the tin on the
scales, and remove spoonfuls until it weighs
½ lb less.)
4 oz (115 g) margarine
Approx. ½ pkt of Rice Krispies
Chocolate

Put the syrup and margarine into a large saucepan, bring to the boil, and continue boiling it for two minutes.

Remove pan from heat, and stir in the Rice Krispies. Mix this well, and spread it in a suitable tin, pressing it well down and smoothing it with the back of a tablespoon.

Melt some chocolate, and pour it over the mixture in the tin. Allow the whole thing to cool and set, then cut it into squares. Keeps well in an airtight, plastic box.

Once on board, start the day well filled

A good full breakfast makes a lot of sense if you are starting a day's boating, even though in port or at home you might normally have no more than a cup of coffee and a roll, or tea and toast.

When you're afloat, add at least some kind of cereal, if you'd rather not cook, but hot food is really the best thing, unless the weather is unusually warm. The reason behind this is simple; even if you aren't one of the stagger-about-on-deck-changing-headsails type of crew, the swing and sway of the boat will keep your body muscles constantly exercising, so you will need considerably more energy (and therefore food) than most people require ashore. And it may not be easy to stoke up later on in the day if the going gets rough.

At breakfast, however, egg dishes (the yolks being sulphurous and extremely rich) are less than ideal if anyone is likely to become squeamish before the day is out. Eggs can actually promote seasickness. Bacon and sausages, tending to be fatty, are better grilled than fried, as the fat runs out into the grill-pan.

In many ways, good old-fashioned porridge is the best thing of all, *if cooked for long enough*. It uses very little gas, if you let it cook itself – in a vacuum flask overnight.

The ingredients (1 part rolled oats, 3 parts water, to 1 pinch of salt) are used thus:

The evening before, bring water and oats slowly to the boil in a pan, stirring continuously. When it is boiling, stir in the salt.

Heat the inside of a wide-necked vacuum jar with hot water from the kettle, tip it out (back into the kettle if you like), then pour the boiling porridge into the jar, leaving a little space at the top, and secure the lid.

By morning, the porridge will have cooked itself gently to creamy, delicious perfection. Milk can be added, when serving, as well as sugar or salt (depending on where you were brought up), but when milk is difficult to get, we used to make the whole mix-up a bit on the runny side, so that it could be eaten without.

Be civilised

Whenever possible, serve food to children at the cabin table. If there's a little motion or *slight* angle of heel, a few dampened tea towels make excellent non-slip mats which stop things skidding about. Glasses and mugs should have broad bases, so that they won't easily fall over.

And for those occasions when the motion is too violent for polite dining, we found again and again that a set of big, one-pint mugs were infinitely better than bowls, when it came to eating off one's knee in the cockpit. Stew, or baked beans with hot-dog sausages mixed in, or other sustaining 'hold-you-down' storm-dishes, can be devoured from the depths of such a mug with a spoon. And big mugs like that have another great advantage in foul weather; they make excellent hand-warmers, easily held without burning your fingers if need be, and their high sides (which is where they score every time over bowls) keep the contents warm right down to the last dregs.

Storing fresh food

Nowadays, what with synthetic resin glues and fibreglass, most modern craft are relatively leak-free, so the dry storage of packet foods such as cereal, flour, cornflour, salt, baking powder, and the many packet-meals is easier than it was. But one mustn't be fooled; sea air is just as moist as ever it was. Plastic containers, which have no inherent smell of their own, are the answer – so long as you can air them periodically.

Eggs are best kept in the sort of polystyrene-foam packs, which usually clip shut – these particular packs give remarkable protection even if they do start whizzing back and forth in the locker.

Fresh meats, fish (unless pulled out of the water for immediate consumption), and dairy products, should of course be kept in a 'fridge, ice-box, or one of those little cooler things that work on the evaporation principle, if you run to that sort of gadgetry. Failing that, keep such goods in the coldest and best ventilated locker in the ship.

Vegetables also need somewhere airy and cool, but don't forget they're there, or they'll probably remind you in rather a nasty manner in due course.

Storing tinned goods

If you have enough small lockers, a good idea is to keep one of them for canned and packet soups, another for assorted processed meats and tins of vegetables, and somewhere else again for the sweets and puddings.

This system has two advantages, the first being that if an inadvertent soaking removes all the labels, you will still be able to have fairly sensible meals, instead of haphazardly opening what turns out perhaps to be pears with steak chunks, or some other unlikely combination of canned astonishments, picked at random from what is left. The second, more useful benefit is when you are selecting the menu for normal meals each day; using this system each 'course' of the meal will be found in a separate locker, saving much rummaging in dark and awkward corners. It makes life a lot easier if there's any sea running!

If you only have large lockers, and can't divide them, try stowing the soups at one end, and sweets at the other, with something obvious, like egg-packings, spare tea towels, or whatever, separating these from the meats and vegetables.

Keeping the various assortments apart like this makes it easier to see when stocks of a particular kind are getting low.

Disposing of the remains

In most places, seagulls do a great clean-up job, thank goodness, but it's worth looking to see if any are around and watching hopefully, before you actually heave left-overs into the water – and even then, there are some surprisingly fussy eaters who will fly down and for no apparent reason turn up their beaks at some seemingly delectable morsel, which is then left bobbing about, polluting the surface of the harbour or bay.

If the things you throw are anyway going to vanish quickly of their own accord and by the action of the water and nature's biochemistry (things like bread, meat and vegetables, scraps, etc.), it won't much matter if they aren't immediately snapped up by a gull, but it's as well to remember that many sensible ports, and most marinas, have extremely strict laws about NOT flinging *any*thing overboard. The foregoing remarks therefore refer mainly to more remote, natural anchorages.

We always avoid dropping things overside anywhere that dries out at Low Water, for obvious reasons. And we made a Ship's Rule that orange-peel (bio-degradable though it is, in time) should *always* be taken ashore, or at least sunk in tins in deep water outside the anchorage or harbour. Orange peel, because of its pith, floats around for ages, and looks really horrid sculling about in the corners of harbours, or drifting onto beaches.

Plastic bags we *never ever throw overboard* now. Not since the day one got round our outboard's propeller and put us and our 27ft catamaran in a very dangerous situation. To clear it, after it stalled the engine, we had to tilt the motor, remove the prop altogether, and pare the stuff off the stub of the shaft, then replace the screw and get under way again – all with a strong tide setting us rapidly onto jagged rocks in a flat calm and heavy swell. You don't forget *that* sort of lesson!

We have several friends who have experienced the acute inconveniences of 'polybags' having been sucked up their engine cooling-water intakes, toilet intakes, and wound around propellers far more deep and inaccessible than ours. Useful though we all know it is, plastic is in many ways the curse of modern society; bags, bottles, boxes, packing materials litter just about every single beach in the world, from the Sands of Par to Polynesia – and that's only from the stuff that's already come ashore . . .

Bins

So, how to get rid of it, not to mention all the other tins and cartons and packages we daily discard? Naturally, if one's next port of call is a harbour or marina where refuse skips or bins will be available, it is an easy matter to retain your oddments of plastic and paper and tins and bottles until you get there. We used pedal-bin liner bags, which even over a couple of days could be retained on board with one of those little wire 'Freezer-bag Ties' closing them tight for safety and sensitive noses. Being small, such bags are easy to carry ashore and dump into the appropriate receptacles.

Bonfires

If one cruises to the wilder, more remote places, such as the superb natural anchorages of the West Coast of Scotland or Ireland, disposing of one's rubbish is more of a problem. We used two methods.

The first was to collect any burnable items (plastic and paper – but not the 'tetra-pack' type of milk carton, which has an inner layer of metal foil), and again in a pedal-bin liner, we'd take them ashore in some suitably deserted spot to burn them at Low Water.

If you are careful to light your little bonfire well below the High Water mark (and enough ahead of a rising Flood so that it won't get quenched before all is burnt), no harm will be done to the environment, and no trace left to offend those who may come after. One has to watch out that dry grasses, heather and the like are well away, or not downwind, lest sparks ignite the surrounding countryside. But there is a further nicety worth mentioning, which is the unpleasant smell of the oily smoke which burning plastic inevitably gives off. One doesn't want it to blow across the water towards other craft sharing your anchorage, any more than one would like it to blow inland to disturb the inhabitants of any near-by dwellings.

We found such small bonfires could be burnt fairly discreetly for the most part, and we tried to make a habit, once we had got it properly going, of scouring the surrounding shoreline for further bits of unsightly refuse left there by the tide. By burning that up too, if one ever was challenged by a local person, one could justifiably claim to be tidying up the environment, not making a mess of it.

Burials at sea

Tins, and bottles, in such out-of-the-way places, cause much more of a problem. Ever since the time our trusty CQR anchor unexpectedly dragged in a light breeze, we have always been careful never to throw empty tins overboard in anchorages; the point of our anchor, on reaching the seabed, had inserted itself in an empty tin, and was thus unable to dig in and hold in the normal manner.

Our ritual for the Committal to the Deep of Tins goes thus: Having opened and emptied the tin in the usual way, we use a beer-can opener (the sort with which you lever a small triangular hole in the end of the can) to puncture its base. (A marlin spike will do.) If you look for the strip of lead which runs down the side of the tin, and bang your hole in the base near that, the tin will always turn 'hole down' in the water and sink quickly when you lob it overside – otherwise it may float for a long time simply because the tin has rolled the hole in its end clear of the waterline.

FIG. 11

DISPOSING OF TINS AT SEA

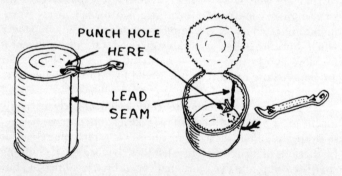

So, having punctured the right part of its bottom, we then flatten the open mouth of the top of the tin – and only then do we consider it ready for Burial At Sea. This flattening has two purposes; first, it stops the can rolling along the seabed too easily, and more importantly, *should* anyone anchor near where it rests, with its mouth closed the danger of a repetition of what happened to us is minimised.

Of course, like everyone else who thinks about these things, we always *try* to remember to sink our empty tins and glass (not plastic) bottles when on passage out at sea. But we don't always remember. If anchoring that night possibly in some unspoilt spot where no 'bin-man' has ever been heard of, let alone seen, we then load our bag of sinkables into the dinghy, and row off either to just outside the entrance, or through into some part inaccessible to yachts, and there sink our flattened and punctured tins. Glass bottles we fill with seawater and screw the caps back on before sinking them. Have you ever noticed the amazing number of screw-caps that manage to float up beaches?

7

The Growing Child
– and Things to Do

Since many small children who come cruising seem to prefer the cabin to the cockpit, when the ship is under way, except perhaps in very calm, sunny weather, they can easily become bored. Obviously Mother shouldn't be expected to spend all her sailing hours down below reading stories, though that certainly can be a rewarding way of getting the very young to settle down quietly, now and then. One has to be able to leave them alone at least for a few minutes occasionally.

If however the below-decks layout of the boat permits the children to play where they can easily see something of their parents out in the cockpit, and especially if they can see the passing scenery if they want to, so much the better, because they are then less likely to feel 'left all alone'. From this point of view, there is a very great deal to be said for the sort of motor-sailer which has a large deckhouse saloon cum wheelhouse, because everyone is then more or less together most of the time. The important thing is to try and ensure that there are plenty of the right sort of toys, games, and other occupations of a relatively safe nature, to keep the youngster interested.

Cuddly toys and boat-toys

When packing our boat-gear for a weekend on board or any longer, we felt it almost as vital not to forget to bring that special 'soul-mate' of each of our daughters, whether it was a battered old teddy or a threadbare but once fluffy pink cot-blanket, without which the respective owners would have felt outrageously deprived and lonely, as it was to remember the owners themselves.

By accidentally leaving a precious animal of some kind on board as we loaded up again for the return trip home, we discovered that it is well worth leaving a particular soft toy to 'look after the ship' in one's absence. The advantage is two-fold. Not only does it mean less to carry to and fro each time; such a toy is *always* there, waiting to produce a happy smile of renewed acquaintance each time its young owner returns. It will also act as a merciful stand-by in case some other precious toy is forgotten in the last-minute rush.

Later on, those particular 'boat-toys' will probably become the guardians of hundreds of happy memories of early days afloat. Our eldest daughter still treasures a now less than white cuddly synthetic seal-pup, whose soft friendship accompanied her on every childhood cruise, sharing the rough and tumble of the Minches, journeying with her to the Hebridean island whose name Rona bears. He, like his owner, has felt the summer sun and crispness of early and late season breezes in the cockpits of three successive yachts, and has often been held up to watch the cavortings on and off near-by rocks of real live creatures of his own kind. And his brown glass eyes, half hidden yet under the white fur of his brow, seem to reflect those scenes to this day.

Among favourite soft toys, when our three were very young, was a light but furry ball about the size of a small grapefruit. At one time it had a sort of bell inside, but long after that had gone silent for internal reasons unknown, the ball itself proved a grand boat-toy, as it could be thrown quite hard all about the cabin (except when meals were being cooked) without fear of harm or hurt to it or to people or equipment.

Sets are a good idea

Rag-dolls with numerous changes of dress were highly popular with our ship-load of girls, but the smaller in scale the better, and this also applied later on to the plastic kind of doll, who had lots of clothes and riding boots and other bits and pieces to add on or take off.

Toys of that kind are most useful, in that they are fairly time-consuming and exercise the mind, but unless the scale is very small, one is forever falling over – or far worse, treading on and breaking – the various bits. Somehow the smaller they are the tougher they seem to be – and the more likely they are to be kept in one place in a box or bag.

For the young child, a simple set of building bricks gives endless fun if they have in the assortment a few interesting arches and so on. Not the interlocking kind; just ordinary old-fashioned wooden blocks. Kits like *Lego*, marvellous though they are, can be hellish in a small ship, as can other similar tiny-component construction kits, because one is forever finding them in unlikely places. Even so, we admit that they may prove worth while for the amount of peace they can create!

One of the most useful and popular toys we came across consisted of a set of tiny wooden farm animals, complete with farmer and family, farmhouses, and the local village. The biggest buildings, which were the two 'Town Halls' (we had two sets) with clocktowers, were no larger than match-boxes, so the whole thing took up very little room when tidied away; but it could be spread out into a table-top world in which many an hour was spent herding the microscopic cattle through winding streets, while un-noticed around it all, the yacht swayed her way across some mighty Firth, or ran at speed towards a distant isle.

The problem of toy stowage

Keeping everything small helps a lot, but if one is to avoid having toys continually scattered all over the ship, and more dangerously over the cabin floor, a proper place must be found for them when not in use.

If each set of things is given its own cloth bag (of a kind that can't cause suffocation if it is worn in play), then supposing the 'farm', or the miniature 'Action Man' outfit is required, its entire set-up can be tipped out – *and put back later*. If just one large play-bag is used, or a locker chosen for all toys to be kept in, the various tiny bits and pieces get lost in the depths or caught up in other things, so a number of smaller bags for the individual kinds of toy are better, and are easier to stow.

Despite good intentions, children are nearly always given the forecabin to play in, or at least to sleep in, and in most small yachts, it will be a fairly easy matter to construct a broad shelf over the foot of the bunks there, with a sufficiently high fiddle-rail to keep everything from Panda to *Pick-a-Stick* in place in a seaway.

Shelves are anyway better than lockers for toys, much though parents might prefer to have them out of sight. Few lockers in small boats are in any case big enough!

A certain tidiness discipline is *essential* at sea, for safety reasons. If things are left lying around they can cause injury. Just one slip on some rolling object that shouldn't have been left on the cabin floor can be disastrous, and no-one *wants* to sit down suddenly and break something when the vessel does an unexpected lurch.

Fortunately, most children enjoy making a bit of ceremony about things traditional. If therefore from the start, one takes care to explain about there being an old, old Rule in ships which says 'A place for everything, and everything in its place', they soon accept the idea that whatever they get away with at home, on board the boat putting their toys back where they belong after playing with them is just like Father putting his navigation instruments and charts back where *they* belong.

Colouring

Most children get considerable fun out of colouring, so a stock of colouring books is a valuable addition to the toy list. Crayons, though admittedly never as attractively brilliant in effect to the small child, are infinitely preferable to watercolour paints or felt-pens, both of which can (and will) make an appalling mess of the furnishings. And that is an important point to remember if holidaying on a chartered yacht!

Table games

Apart from a twin pack of playing-cards allowing for everything from *Happy Families* and *Canasta* to *Patience* as well as card-house construction (in the right weather conditions!), board-games of one kind or another can be a great boon on board.

The cheapest and most compact way to get variety, is to buy a good-quality *Compendium of Games*, comprising things like *Snakes & Ladders*, *Draughts*, *Chess*, *Ludo*, and *Dominoes*. Good solid pieces and stout boards are worth the extra outlay.

Complicated games like *Monopoly* are something of a problem, partly because the risk of losing essential parts is considerable, but more because of the length of time they take to play.

A couple of spare dice may come in handy.

Dinghy race

We adapted the idea of another game which in the published form had a confusion of rather complicated Rules, to make our own much more simple *Dinghy Race* board-game. Over the years this has proved amazingly popular, not only with our family, but with guests and charterers of all ages too, so we think it worth describing here in some detail.

It consists of squared paper, pasted (with waterproof glue) to a cardboard back, on which the family artist painted the irregular shoreline of a lake around the edges, with little headlands here and there, and one or two pronounced bays of reasonably broad indentation elsewhere. (See p. 132.)

A Club Quayside was painted on, towards one corner of the South end of the lake, its face on an East-West line; and then parallel to it and five squares off, out in the water, a Starting Line of suitable length was drawn, with a buoy painted at each end of it. Numbered squares along the face of the Quay represented berths for each of the dinghies (made from cut-up bits of india-rubber erasers which fitted the squares, and into which thin cardboard mainsails (individually coloured) were stuck, complete with Sail Numbers which corresponded to the Quay berth numbers.

There was a Wind Arrow, to be placed on a marked compass rose on the land in a corner of the board, initially indicating a Northerly wind, the direction of which will be altered as the game proceeds.

There was also an irregularly shaped island more or less in the middle, which also had headlands, some with reefs of separate rocks extending a short way out, so that it would be just possible for lucky boats to short-cut inside the odd gap in them on occasion.

Buoys, each fully occupying one square, were painted in as Course Markers, 'A'-buoy a little way into a bay at the far end of the lake from the starting line, and (to make it fair) directly opposite the centre of that line. 'B'-buoy was right off to the left-hand side of the lake a bit more than half-way back down, and the course from it to 'C'-buoy could be sailed variously around several smaller islands placed rather in the way but with enough clear water between them not to cramp things unduly. 'C'-buoy itself was put about a quarter of the way up the first leg of the course (from the middle of the starting line to 'A'-buoy).

An Olympic-type course would be sailed; from the Start to A, to B, to C, up the board again to A and then directly back down it and straight across the line to finish. To add interest, there were various groups of squares covered with painted ripples, each group extending over quite a few squares in assorted patterns, and collectively these groups barred any attempt to sail in a direct straight line from one mark to another.

There was then a small pack of Hazard cards which we made up, some nice and some nasty; so that a player sailing onto a Ripple square took a card – which read, for instance: '*Capsize – miss 2 turns*', or '*On the plane – continue 6 squares in same direction*' (which could be awkward if something was in the way up ahead), '*Centre-plate jammed up – drift 2 squares directly downwind*', '*Useful squall, take an extra turn*', '*Wind veers 45°*', '*Aground on surprise shoal – miss 1 turn*', '*Wind backs 90°*', and so on.

To play, each person in turn threw the single die until all had achieved different scores and were thus allotted a boat number,

MAKE YOUR OWN "DINGHY RACE"

BOARD GAME

FIG. 12

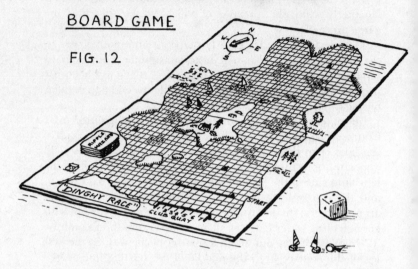

that with the lowest Sail Number always making the first real move away from the corresponding number at the Quayside. Each turn had to be made in a straight line only, one square per dot on the dice, either diagonally, or up-or-down or across the squares. The only restriction to this (apart from land, other boats, and of course a Mark of the Course) just as in real racing, was the Wind Direction, directly into which one naturally cannot sail, so that one was forced to tack along at 45 degrees to it, if trying to work to windward.

The square directly in front of another boat was 'out of bounds' even in passing, if that boat was on Starboard Tack (wind coming over its right-hand side) and the other was on Port Tack. Going aground meant missing 1 turn, but hitting a mark of the course or another boat meant missing 3 turns – definitely to be avoided!

To represent the effect of a real yacht race's Five Minute Gun, on leaving the Quay, each boat had to take a total of *three* turns before starting across the line. If you went over the line too soon, you had to return before being allowed to continue up the board towards 'A'-buoy, just as in the real thing. The game was always good fun, because it was never the same twice, and fortunes would wax and wane from moment to moment.

As reading abilities improve with the years, one can of course add to the games repertoire with *Lexicon*, *Junior Scrabble*, and then the senior version, a 'travel pack' of which with its pegged letters is ideal; but long before that, once numbers had been mastered, games of *Battleships* requiring only pencils and paper, had often been played with 'shots' fired verbally from bunk to bunk as the adults sailed the (real) vessel across the open seas.

We got many excellent ideas from the paperback *Dictionary of Games* by J.B. Pick, published by J.M. Dent & Sons, a volume which has well proved its worth to us, both at home and afloat.

Fishing

We were never happy about small children using proper fishing tackle, because we have witnessed more than one nasty incident with fish-hooks through fingers etc. There are however several safe forms of fishing; that in rock-pools with little shrimping nets being one – and our kids' 'nets-on-sticks' have several times been the instant means of rescuing small items inadvertently thrown overboard.

A very popular form of 'fishing' can be achieved inside a yacht's cabin, using a short stick, piece of line, small magnet, and assorted steel nuts and washers. The latter are placed on the cabin floorboards at the foot of the companion steps, and the rod/line/magnet combination is taken up into the hatchway, from where the 'fishing' takes place, in turns with a time-limit, so a score can be kept. If the boat is rolling or pitching a little, it greatly adds to the fun and expertise!

Trailing 'porpoises'

Trailing things astern, as mentioned on page 76, can be an absorbing pastime too. We initially beachcombed a few assorted small fishing floats, and towed these many a happy mile on lengths of line, watching them dip, bob, and bounce in our wake. (The thing to remember is to bring them back inboard before putting the engine into reverse . . .)

We know of a family who used to tow their fenders in this way for fun, having found that the shape of modern plastic inflated fenders makes their behaviour at different speeds quite spectacular. They hit on the lovely idea, too, of 'personalising' them by drawing faces on them with 'indelible' marker pens, so that each of the crew had his own. Regrettably said faces became printed on the topsides of another yacht alongside which they had spent the following night in port!

Nautical fun – the first instruction

Bits and pieces from the bosun's locker can be interesting for kids. A game of joining shackles together, or tying complicated knots in assorted rope ends (*not* the jibsheets!) passes many a merry while, and right from a very early age, we instilled an elementary understanding of navigation by having a coloured chart of the cruising area, and showing the children where we were on it from time to time during the day, always starting by pointing out where we had spent the previous night. This of course meant that before long they got a mental picture of where on the chart the best beaches were. And every time we looked like nearing one, there would be something of an outcry if we couldn't for some reason stop for a while. With several children on board one can organise competitions to identify charted features. This can make chartwork fun even at quite an early age.

Shore and shallows

We carried a supply of buckets and spades on board to begin with, and those plastic rings or discs you throw and try to catch. The best fun however, once the toddler age was just past, was *bathing with lifejackets on*. The girls soon learned that they could float around securely in the shallows, under our watchful eyes, and *we* soon learned if a lifejacket was not fitting or doing its job as well as it ought.

Another popular pastime, before they could row themselves in the dinghy, was being rowed by a parent into the shallows surrounding an anchorage, and if the sea was clear, drifting about in a few inches of water or close among the rocks, while peering over the gunwale to watch hermit crabs, tube-worms, and other intriguing sea-creatures living out their lives below. The transparent-bottomed miniature paddling pool which we used as a baby-bath on board made this especially interesting in *very* shallow pools, and as a result, the whole family has gradually developed a considerable interest in marine life.

Helping on deck

There is no point in trying to get a child to steer, if he isn't big enough to see over the cabintop. But as soon as he *can* see where he's going, it is quite amazing how quickly a youngster can pick up the necessary skill. The smaller the boat, the more interesting steering is likely to be for him, because the time which elapses between his putting the helm over, be it by wheel or tiller, and the head of the boat beginning to turn, will be less. And it goes without saying that a well-balanced boat will be easier to manage for small, lightweight people, than one which pulls their arms out.

We allowed our girls to try their hands at steering compass courses very early on, and they all picked up the ability very quickly; but as with all young children, concentration would only last for relatively few minutes, and they would then get bored and want to do something else.

Many parents will naturally tend to hand over the helm to their little ones when the boat is well clear of any obstruction or other craft, and preferably well out in open water where they are unlikely to hit anything: understandable, but, as we discovered, not a good idea. The tyro helmsman is much more able to relate to the effect of his helm movements if he can see the boat turning against some *near-by* feature of land – something not more than a couple of hundred yards away.

So, staying close to them if you must, but trying your level best not actually to put a hand on the tiller or wheel yourself, let them steer through some relatively narrow channel, just as soon as you think they have mastered the ability to turn the boat and straighten her up again. You can then 'con' them by word of mouth – they won't mind that, so long as they can feel it is *they* who are actually steering, and not you.

Up on the West Coast of Scotland, near Crinan, there is a stretch of water where the tide sweeps through between numerous rocks and islands at between 7 and 8 knots. The overfalls and general surface disturbances are enough to swing a yacht this way and that at times, and our young ones used to love steering through this bit each time we passed that way. Just holding the boat on course, away out miles from anywhere, was deemed deadly boring by comparison, because the satisfaction to be gained from meeting and checking the action of each wave, so as to leave a ruler-straight wake effortlessly hissing out astern, is one that comes only after a very great deal of practice.

Flying the flags

From very early days, a child can learn to hoist and lower the ship's ensign; later on they can reliably secure the flag to the halyard as well, and thus do the whole operation. The masthead burgee too can soon become manageable, though the skipper will no doubt have to untangle the flagstick from the rigging many times before the knack is correctly learned.

Once these skills have been mastered, a child will like to feel that the flag (or any part of the ship's gear that he can manage on his own) is his responsibility at the beginning and end of each day, or whenever adjustment is needed. The routine of taking in the flags at sunset (9 p.m., whichever comes first, to be pedantic), apart from being another ancient maritime tradition to live up to, makes him feel 'required' as part of the crew, rather than just a passenger.

While handling the ropes of sails may be rather too much (and too dangerous) for a small child for several years, helping to stow the headsail in its bag, possibly un-hanking it from the stay as well, can soon enough be managed. For this sort of thing, though, some sort of headgear may be advisable, to avoid the risk of fine long hair blowing about and getting caught in the gear.

Come on, you swabs!

After the muddy anchor has been brought inboard at the start of a passage, or the grit of a harbour has been left astern, there's always the fun of swabbing down the decks with a mop or brush, while someone else swooshes buckets of cold seawater over one's toes. But until a child is quite sizeable and strong, it would be foolish to let him try to fill a bucket over the side when the boat is moving or in a tideway. If the weight of water isn't enough to pull him overboard, the drag of the bucket almost certainly will, if he hasn't the presence of mind to let go first – another bucket lost overboard!

The knack of swinging the bucket forward, when the boat is moving, so that it hits the water ahead of the thrower, fills (a small weight attached to the rim at one side will ensure this), and is then hoisted clear of the water just as it arrives below you, is one that requires a degree of understanding and anticipation, as well as physical strength, and is best not attempted for quite a few years.

Help with the sails

The same applies to the hoisting and setting of sails. Until a person is big and strong enough to achieve the final tightness required, there is little point in letting him 'do it on his own', because there is nothing so soul-destroying than to do something as well as you can, and immediately see somebody undo it and do it up harder. Far better, once children begin to want to help making sail, is to get them to do the heaving up until the last bit, and then with suitable thanks, ask them to stand clear while you firm it up. They'll understand that this calls for more strength than they possess.

A boat which has a small sail like a mizzen or an inner

staysail, has an advantage, since a child can be put in charge of something of the sort, once he has been taught to set, adjust, sheet, and lower and finally stow it correctly. It really won't be long before your growing crew can manage the boat on their own, and the parents become mere passengers.

Children on passage

Inevitably the family cruising boat will sooner or later make a sea-passage of more than just a few hours' duration, be it simply to reach a particular cruising-ground, or to get home on time after being delayed by bad weather. But even if it is just an extended day's sail of fifty miles or so, it is likely to be much less interesting to the very young than it is to their parents. Timing the passage so that they sleep through it has its advantages.

As children grow and need less sleep, they might be allowed to stand a night watch along with an adult. If they are capable of holding the boat on a compass course even for a few minutes now and then, or can act as lookout, aid navigation by counting the flashes of buoys and so on, they can be made to feel really useful and responsible when still quite small, and the experience is one which they will long remember and (hopefully) cherish, and will certainly be the source of many a tale to tell back at school.

The important thing will be to see that they are really warmly dressed and wind-proofed, wearing a safety harness, and also, to keep them occupied. Making suitable notes in the deck-log, checking the burgee with the torch for the helmsman's benefit (after being told not to shine it on nearby parts of the deck to avoid blinding everyone), reading the log on the hour, and fetching the biscuits, are all things a young watch-keeper can do perfectly well with practice, and part of getting him to do these jobs will ensure that he won't get chilled through total inactivity or queasiness.

But the real advantage in allowing a child to do the occasional night watch after dark and normal bedtime, is that he or she may then be glad enough of a lie-in next morning, after the destination has been reached.

Useful fun

Our youngsters began playing with odd bits of line and rope ends at a very early age, and an interest in knot-tying can be quite easily sparked off. We recall tying a figure-eight knot in a bit of light line, and challenging the girls to see if any of them could make a copy of it at the other end. This achieved, it was possible to go on to show how to tie the two ends of the line together, how to tie a clove-hitch around a stanchion or some other suitable object, and finally to work up to that fourth most useful knot of all, the bowline.

For the bowline, we had most success by teaching the amusing rabbit-hole story, where you make a loop, the standing part of the line being the 'tree', so that the 'rabbit', the end of the line held in the hand, is made to pop up out of the 'hole', dash round the back of the tree (see the farmer coming), and dive back down the hole. One can do so much with a simple bowline or two – tying ropes to fittings, or joining a couple of different ropes together – that the knot is perhaps the best of all to know really well. And once it has been done 'without looking' a few times, a child can safely be left to secure dinghy painters, fenders, and even the ship herself, so long as there is no strain on the rope while the knot is being tied. Obviously there are better knots for these jobs, but a bowline *can* in certain circumstances be used for almost anything.

The annual re-fit

The job of scrubbing the ship's bottom was also looked on as part of crewing. And because it was a messy business, it especially appealed to the young.

Sanding the hull down after scrubbing was also quite enjoyed, and it was sometimes amazing how much real care went into doing it, particularly when working round fiddling skin fittings like the log impeller and the ship's propeller. The skipper, of course, had to remember each year to give instructions about how to deal with special bits, such as the exposed echo-sounder transducer head – if he didn't, it would inevitably get sanded and painted like everything else – including the crew.

Poisonous paints

Antifouling paints are often exceedingly poisonous, and the thinners may be even worse, so for this reason we turned a very deaf ear on the many pleas to be allowed actually to slap on paint, until we were quite sure the children were old enough and responsible enough to avoid getting it in their mouths or eyes. Even then, we kitted them out first in old oilskins and other disposable gear, covering their hair with hoods and their hands with those transparent disposable gloves of the thin, almost 'un-feelable' sort bought by the package. These precautions proved to have been very worth while.

Once the technique of brushing the paint on quickly in panels one after another along the boat's side had been mastered, with a good width of masking tape at the waterline, we adults were happy to find that there was no obvious difference between the bits we'd done (admittedly in half the time) and those the children had spread about. And since ours was a purely cruising boat, with not much worry about achieving a 'racing finish', it all proved satisfactory enough, and everyone had fun, even the youngest having done their bit before wandering off to play.

Naturally we did not use power tools or electric sanders on that open beach. But even had electricity been available, and we had been fitting out in some nice dry shed and not over puddles, we would certainly not have allowed the children to use such tools until we considered them responsible enough. The risks to the boat, never mind to our youngsters, would have been far too high!

The captain's word . . .

As with the job of painting ship, so with everything else to do with any size or shape of boat, be she a ten-foot dinghy or an ocean liner, it is vital that any instruction, request, or order given by the person in charge, should be obeyed at once. Children have to be told this right from the start, and its importance explained.

While discipline may be one thing back on land, it really is crucially important afloat, for the safety of all concerned. And because safety is involved, there can be no time for questions or hesitations. Being human, children like to know there really is a reason behind any order an adult might give them — even though they might not be particularly interested in hearing the precise details. We made a point of explaining whenever possible why this or that order had been (or preferably, was about to be) given, but we made quite sure our junior crew knew that there would be plenty of occasions when there might well be no time to explain, let alone ask a second time, and that therefore any order barked at them in an urgent tone of voice *must* be acted upon instantly. And they were always very good about it, as long as we were afloat. At home they argued the toss as usual, mostly.

When our three were very young, however, they had several times asked their mother *why* Daddy had stopped them doing this or that with no seemingly obvious reason, and her stock reply used to be: 'Because Daddy is the Skipper, and in a ship the Skipper's word is Law'.

So for years afterwards, when some peculiar and inexplicable order was issued by the Master of *our* ship, it would be obeyed, but invariably with a shrug and a cheery sigh: 'Daddy's the 'Kipper!'

8

Young Crew Members

To begin with, children have neither the weight nor the strength to do much that is really useful aboard a cruising yacht, but as they grow to reasonable proportions, say around the age of eight or ten, they can usually take a much more active part in the running of the ship. Dinghy work, deck, and even anchor work to some extent, handling sails and helm in moderate winds, and the basic arts of navigation can all be managed.

This, then, is when the parents can happily hand over to their youngsters for short periods, both in daylight and on passage after dark – provided they have taught carefully and allowed their growing crew to try everything for themselves without being hovered over too noticeably. Skippers who like to strive for perfectly set sails and faultless handling under sail might be hesitant to allow their youngsters to help, lest they make a mess of things. This would be a pity for, in normal circumstances, on-the-job training with minimum interference makes for a remarkably keen and proficient young crew.

As explained in the last chapter, there are things like dealing with flags and other light jobs which can be handed over to the youngsters at quite an early age, but youth demands to be taught real skills, so that they can feel truly proud of their efforts, and perhaps the most useful of these is the handling of dinghies.

As with all family boating, it is vital not to lose sight – in one's desire to impress the learner with the need to do things the correct way – of the fact that it is all supposed to be *fun*. Obviously if a child feels 'made to do' whatever job is involved, he or she may instantly rebel, and either refuse to take any further interest in it, or possibly take to hating the whole business of boating from that moment on. In your mind and theirs, therefore, this section should really come under the heading of 'Water Sports'.

First dinghy arts

The point to emphasise about dinghies is that all the family, young and old, should be wearing a properly secured lifejacket before embarking.

We think that probably the best way to show a child how to row is for one adult to take one child alone in the dinghy. It will be better not to take along anyone else, so as to avoid the learner being bombarded with other advice or ribald comments from siblings.

A short, lightweight dinghy will be better than a long heavy one, for although the latter kind may row far better and in a straighter line, the longer, heavier oars may prove too much for a featherweight rower.

Our daughter Eileen, aged only three, had her first lesson at the oars of a six-foot inflatable. Even its light paddles were sufficiently heavy to lift her little bottom right off the seat each time she attempted to raise the blades from the water at the end of a stroke. In the end her tutor had to sit so that her adult legs held down Eileen's, in order that progress (even round and round) could be achieved. In time, Eileen learned not to 'windmill', and how to use the weight of her shoulders and back to assist with the pulling, and became an extremely competent oarsman who could leave a nice double line of bubbles in a fine straight line across any anchorage.

For the first few strokes, with the adult in the stern facing the beginner, both sets of hands can be applied to the oars, until some sort of rhythm of the '– reach – in – pull – out – and reach forward again –' sort, becomes fairly automatic. Once the learner can manage to string together as many as three or four consecutive strokes, Stage Two may be tried.

Solo, on a long line

Stage Two consists of securing a long, light rope such as a spare spinnaker halyard, to the stern of the anchored or moored parent vessel, and its other end to the stern (NOT the bow) of the dinghy. The learner is then sent off completely solo with the oars. If there is any wind at all, or any current worth mentioning, the dinghy will inevitably drift astern, and the rower is told to try and make his or her way back.

Being securely tethered, even if an oar goes adrift, the dinghy and its occupant can safely be hauled back to the yacht (or shore, since this same method can be used, hitching the end of the line for instance to a jetty, if no parent vessel is available).

The point about tying the dinghy-end of the line to its stern, rather than its bow, is so that the trailing rope will stay clear of the oars as the boat moves forward. If one just uses an extension of the dinghy's normal *bow* painter, the most awful tangles can occur, and the young rower may well be discouraged. Another advantage of the line trailing from the dinghy's stern is that the drag of the line will assist the beginner to row straight, whereas if it is secured instead to the bow, it may tend to keep turning the head of the dinghy to one or other side.

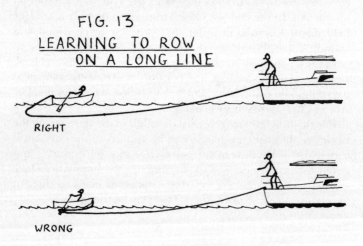

FIG. 13
LEARNING TO ROW
ON A LONG LINE

RIGHT

WRONG

Tie the oars together

If the rowlocks are not of the sort which in any event will prevent the oars from sliding out and overboard, simply tie the looms (handles) of the oars loosely together, using a piece of line of such a length that when the oars are being properly used it will not tighten. The rower will soon appreciate the need not only to control the angle of the oar blades, but to keep the oars themselves steady in the rowlocks, without letting them slide awkwardly in and out at each stroke.

As soon as simple, straightforward rowing has been mastered, teach the rower to make a correct approach to the side of the yacht or jetty, getting him to come in, rowing at an angle of about 45 degrees towards the boat's (jetty's) side, and at the last minute bringing the oar nearest the yacht/jetty inboard, and turning the dinghy parallel, alongside, by backwatering with the oar on the far side.

What if an oar goes overboard?

The danger is that in trying to reach the oar as it drifts away, the dinghy itself might capsize; so it is far better to teach everyone who uses the dinghy on their own how to propel it competently with a single oar.

Granted, different dinghies require different techniques; few inflatable dinghies for example have any provision for single-oar sculling over the stern. In them, the only answer is to kneel in the bow (where stability is at its worst) and scoop your way along with the oar-blade, either by paddling Indian-canoe style a few strokes at a time on alternate sides of the bow, or by using a method similar but opposite to the normal system of sculling over the stern.

Sculling

The most efficient means of single-oar propulsion is probably that of sculling over the transom of a boat equipped with

FIG. 14

1.
HOLD OAR THUS;
BLADE HORIZONTAL
IN WATER. SO THAT
IT CAN EASILY BE
MOVED EITHER WAY.

2.
PUSH WITH
WRIST, BENDING
HAND BACK, TO
TWIST BLADE

3.
AT END OF STROKE
FLEX WRIST TO BEND
HAND FORWARD AND
TWIST BLADE THE
OTHER WAY.

4.
PULL WITH
WRIST. KEEP
HAND BENT
FORWARD.

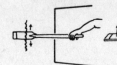
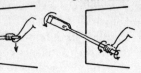

(AT END OF
THIS STROKE
REVERT TO 2.)

1.
2.

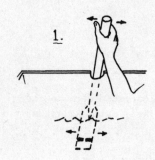
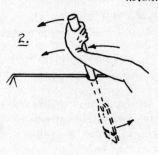

SCULLING

3.
4.

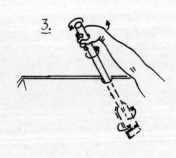
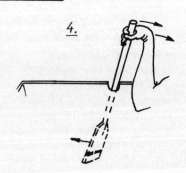

sculling notch or stern rowlock. If the method can be learned, as shown in the diagrams, so much the better, because it is capable of moving a boat along at quite a respectable speed without very much effort, even into quite stiff breezes. And since it is often in troublesome weather conditions that one is most likely to lose an oar in the first place, being able to manoeuvre round and get it back without undue stress or difficulty can be a great asset.

We once broke a dinghy oar when rowing hard into a near gale and trying to get ashore in a hurry, but because we knew how to cope, it took only a moment to shift the remaining oar to the stern and continue, picking up the broken bits on the way. With open water to leeward of us, and night coming on, we might otherwise have been in difficulties.

It could be argued that one should be taught single-oar sculling before two-oar rowing, as a safety precaution, but the trouble is that most young people will learn better if in the boat on their own, and where over-the-stern sculling is being taught, any line linking the dinghy with the shore or a parent vessel will get in the way, so it would seem better to get the young oarsman used to proper rowing first. Once he can safely manage the boat solo in the normal manner, single-oar methods can then be taught without any safety rope getting tangled round the blade in the process.

The finer points come later

Obviously since young people like doing things at the highest possible speed, and enjoy demonstrating their skill to anyone who might be watching, one has an ideal opportunity now of showing them how to 'feather' the oar-blades when rowing conventionally into a fresh breeze. It's only a matter of dropping the wrists, in relation to the hands, each time the oars are pushed away on being lifted clear of the water, so that the oar-blades turn flat, parallel to the water – and of course keeping the blades themselves low down over the water surface on that same stroke, before lifting the wrists, and dipping the blades for the next pull.

The need for a second dinghy

The trouble with teaching the kids to row, is that once they have got hold of the idea that they can manage the dinghy without your help, they immediately want to – all the time.

Some parents won't let their children take out the dinghy alone until they have proved themselves reasonably competent swimmers: this helps the child feel more responsible and the parent more assured. When the children do take out the dinghy on their own, however, the parents will become marooned on board, or ashore, unless a second dinghy of some sort is available. It also means that if, as is quite likely when they're still relatively inexperienced in the dinghy on their own, they get into some sort of difficulty (e.g. can't row back against an increased windspeed), neither mother nor father will be able to render assistance except by shouting at them – which possibly may not help!

At the baby stage, however, the real fear is that one parent might be ashore with the only dinghy when Junior manages to fall overboard and float away. So, having some kind of second dinghy when the children reach this stage of independent boating, is rather more than just desirable. For those families with only a small 'pocket' cruising yacht, to have two dinghies may seem excessive, but in our experience one should nevertheless contrive somehow to take a second 'ship's boat' along. Obviously then, the lighter and simpler it is, the better.

For many years we used a succession of cheap plastic inflatable boats as our 'back-up' dinghies. We kept a sturdier little tub of semi-solid construction which could be rowed hard into a considerable wind and sea, for such jobs as laying out second anchors when bad weather threatened, and for ferrying.

Any sort of two-man inflatable dinghy will do very well as a second dinghy, for the young to play about in. Inflatables have the advantage that if in their youthful enthusiasm (or inexperience) they inadvertently bash into anything, be it a rock, a mooring-buoy, or another craft, little damage will be done, whereas a 'solid' dinghy, whether of plastics or wood, is likely to leave its mark, or to acquire that of whatever it hits. In general, too, most inflatables are pretty stable and more forgiving when it comes to aquatic horseplay, which is bound to occur. Inflatables also make amusing additions to the family's collection of swimming aids. When inverted they make quite acceptable rafts for sunbathing, etc. An even more important point, however, is that compared to most 'solid' dinghies, inflatables are usually quite easy to get into from the water, and can therefore be of vital assistance if anyone should fall overboard from the parent vessel.

When the yacht is under way, the second dinghy may be stowed on cabintop or elsewhere on deck, or perhaps deflated and put in a locker, if you don't wish to tow it. At all events, ours proved worth its weight in gold every time we stopped, becoming a valued addition to our general in-port mobility, and for the highly important sense of freedom it gave to our young crew.

Sailing dinghies as tenders

If one or other of your dinghies can be made to sail, the fun for your children (not to mention their elders, on occasion), can be doubled.

The rig should be such that it takes only a moment to set up, otherwise there may be a tendency not to bother. Any spars should either be jointed, or of such a length that they can be stowed within the dinghy itself. That way even if you carry them on board a parent vessel, they will not take up too much room.

The advantages of sailing dinghies are numerous, apart from the fun they can provide. They are relatively silent compared to dinghies driven by outboard motors. And they are much cheaper to run. More than that, though, is the fact that there is nothing like a small sailing dinghy to teach a youngster quickness of reaction and confidence in boat-handling. The knowledge that once he or she has mastered the ability to manoeuvre such a boat under sail, however tiny and simple her gear may be, he or she will be quite capable of applying the same skill to virtually *any* sailing vessel, is a valuable incentive.

There are many books about how to sail dinghies, from which virtually the entire art may be learned, starting with how to rig the boat and take her out for the first time, and finishing with how to get the best speed and win races in National and International Dinghy Classes.

In the initial stages, however, we would recommend the very simplest books on 'How to Sail'. Few youngsters aged less than about thirteen will otherwise be bothered to plough through anything technical or complex on the subject. (This conviction gave rise to the writing of *Simple Sailing* by Jim Andrews, published in 1975 by World's Work Ltd., with the idea of teaching the absolute novice in the plainest, most concise manner.)

Suitable sailing dinghies

It of course depends on what you wish to do with a dinghy. If she is to be the family's only boat, that is one thing, if the younger members will want to race (eventually) it is another, and if the parents wish to race, another again. Fortunately there is a very wide choice of craft suitable for each of these ideals, as a leisured walk around the Dinghy Section of any major Boat Show will quickly reveal.

For beginning, however, the smaller the boat and less complicated her gear is, the better. And if the boat is to double as a tender for a larger craft like the family cruising boat, then other factors such as light weight, good rowing qualities, and stable, easy towing abilities coupled with ample load carrying, will be the vital factors. It may also be that a folding boat could be worth considering, especially with a view to getting the thing on board the parent vessel during open-water passages.

At the time of writing, there are basically three types of folding sailing dinghy available on the British market, any of which might be suitable. These are the sailing inflatable, the folding wooden dinghy which packs flat when not in use, and the semi-rigid, semi-fabric (and therefore semi-folding) type, with built-in buoyancy. (See pp. 25 & 46.)

Sailing inflatables seem all the rage now, though they tend to be costly for their size and have a relatively short life-expectancy. But they do have the undeniable advantage over solid sailing dinghies that if the tyro helmsman misjudges things when coming alongside, the inflatable bow acts as a buffer. Stopping even the smallest sailing craft in just the right place is a skill mastered only after a number of hearty thumps or total misses, so something with a bit of built-in resilience might be considered to have an advantage over harder, more angular designs.

Be that as it may, a really good solid dinghy is often the best of the lot when it comes to rowing into a wind, or indeed simple sailing for the fun of it, and certainly, if there are two or more children in the family, something like the ubiquitous plywood *Mirror 10* may prove just the thing, even though it would almost certainly have to be towed if used as a yacht tender, rather than carried on board. In total length it is 10ft 10in (3.3 m), and weighs about 100 lb (roughly 45 kg) stripped. (See p. 26.)

Rules about sailing around anchorages

One of the things that parents should explain most carefully to their young, when giving them command of a dinghy, is the set of commonsense and natural courtesy rules which anyone using such a boat in the close vicinity of other craft, should observe.

The first of these is clearly not to make a nuisance of one's self to other people and their boating activities – so much is obvious. But there are less apparent rules, and of these perhaps the most important is *'never to try to pass close across the bow of any anchored or moored craft'* – nor indeed the bows of *any* craft whether she is under way or stationary.

Most boats lying to an anchor, for instance, will point in a given direction either due to the influence of wind or current, whichever has the greater effect. It stands to reason, therefore, that either the wind or the current will try to thrust a dinghy attempting to cross the anchored vessel's bows, down upon them, and if under sail it may not always be easy or possible to tack clear at the last moment. We have watched numerous children miscalculate in this way, and end up entangled. Embarrassing for them, and extremely annoying for the owners of the vessels concerned.

Be considerate

The same thing goes for dinghies being rowed, or driven under outboard engine, when near to other craft. No-one wants to see their carefully maintained topsides scuffed or scratched by careless kids – theirs or others! Nor does anyone want to have the peace of their anchorage shattered by the busy buzzing of an outboard in the hands of some youth joy-riding close past anchored craft with a huge wake in tow.

It is up to the parents to be very strict about this sort of behaviour. It is not after all just a matter of politeness and consideration for others: the wash created even by a small boat being driven near her hull-speed (only about four knots for most yacht tenders) can be considerable, and should someone be below decks, maybe cooking a meal or pouring something hot, just as the wash strikes, the result can be extremely serious. Any child put in charge of a boat with an engine should be made aware of this.

One evening one of us was up in a bosun's chair at the masthead of our 28ft ketch, working on a fitting while a youngster was tearing about our anchorage in a speedboat. Anyone's entitled to a little harmless fun, but the trouble was that he seemed for some reason to enjoy making our vessel roll viciously from side to side, with the inevitable effect at the masthead. Our shouts had no chance of being heard by him, over the much closer whining roar of his power unit, and the thumps and crashes as his boat completed circuit after circuit and leapt and bounced over her own wash. Clinging on as our masthead swung swiftly from side to side became more and more of a strain, and resulted in severe nips and grazes on arms and legs. Fortunately he got bored with the game, but only just in time . . .

Knowing the dangers

Once they have the strength to operate the starting mechanism, quite young children *can* be trained to handle small outboard engines, but because there are very considerable risks associated with the manoeuvring of outboard-powered open dinghies and speedboats, we think a fair stage of good commonsense and reason should have been attained by one's offspring before they should be allowed to go powerboating on their own. Sixteen, the age when (in Britain) they are legally entitled to drive a mo-ped, might be a sensible age to start.

The Golden Rule of powerboating must always be to *take along a pair of oars or paddles.* Engines, particularly in the hands of inexperienced youngsters, can be outrageously unreliable, and tend in the way of man-made things to fail in the most awkward circumstances possible.

The hazard of a sudden sharp turn under power is also well known; many a quick flip thus caused, has ended if not in tragedy, at least in hasty rescue operations and an expensively dunked engine.

Motoring downwind, even in the relatively small, choppy little waves which can build up in a modest-sized bay or lake, can present an even greater risk, not so readily appreciated until the stern comes round out of control, the bow goes down, and boat and occupants are suddenly in all sorts of trouble.

With the very short tiller provided on most small outboard motors, keeping the craft in a straight line is not always an easy matter, and in our experience most beginners tend to over-steer and over-correct, moving the engine this way and that by far too great a margin. It helps a great deal if the first few lessons can be given at fairly low speeds, with the engine well throttled back. Of course, once Junior gets away in the boat on his own, it won't be very long before the natural urge to experiment (and to hell with what Father has just said) will result in trying what it's like at full speed. That, after all and regrettably, is part of growing up!

We tend to keep our dinghy outboard for special long-distance journeys to and from the shore, rather than just for 'fun use' for its own sake, and because it has a definite purpose, most kids will very much enjoy using the motor to ferry parents, fuel cans, water containers and so on, backwards and forwards, and should be encouraged to do so as soon as they are reasonably competent. Which is usually slightly earlier than most fathers will admit.

Mind you, doing these jobs under *sail* is even more fun – when it's possible.

Dinghy games

Having just gone on at length about the risks and irritations of putting kids in sole charge of dinghies, let us redress the balance by returning to the point about having, if at all possible, two ship's boats, for the young to play with.

It will not matter how different the two craft are, either in size or type; the youngsters should have endless fun out of exploring once you are satisfied that they are competent enough to handle the craft in the weather conditions.

Assuming that both dinghies can be spared, such games as 'Dinghy Tug of War', where the two are joined by a stern-line and then rowed away from each other, have to be done with care, and definitely with lifejackets on. A point to watch is that the rope should be attached to some part of the boat which really can stand the considerable strain that can be imposed *in jerks*; this is especially important on inflatables, where most fittings are merely glued in place and can easily be ripped off. Taking the line round a seat might be one way of overcoming this problem.

'Dinghy Tig' also provides endless hilarity, the more so if at least one of the boats is an inflatable. Two of our daughters in the *Puffin* semi-collapsible sailing dinghy (under sail) would chase or be pursued by the third, rowing fit to bust in the *Bagboat* as we called our cheap inflatable. The latter was nothing like so fast as the bigger sailing dinghy, but had the advantage, like Drake snapping at the heels of the Spanish Armada's galleons in his nippy little English ships, of being vastly more manoeuvrable. We had a 9 metre catamaran, which had about two feet of headroom under the bridgedeck between her two slim hulls, and while the *Puffin* would be sailing around the far side of its big mother-ship, smaller sister in the *Bagboat* would come scudding through underneath, to spring out unexpectedly and catch her at the stern.

Making real crews of them

Only when one's children have grown enough to be able to manage not just the dinghy, but a reasonable number of the jobs around the parent vessel as well, will they really begin to enjoy and take a fully active part as crew. So the earlier they can be shown how to do the many jobs entailed in seagoing, the better.

From the age of about twelve, steering, watch-keeping, and even the setting and stowing of quite large sails are all jobs which they can help with or even accomplish unaided – even if the skipper may occasionally have to put up with poorly hoisted or ill-sheeted sails.

Strength, however, is not a necessary requirement for a youngster to be able to pull far more than his or her actual weight. There are many parts that can be played. Someone who can keep the yacht's deck-log written up every hour can be a most valuable aid to the busy skipper/navigator, and navigation itself can be successfully learnt, at least in rudimentary form, at a surprisingly early age.

Teaching the art of pilotage

We found that the best way to get the young interested in navigation was to discuss, with the aid of the chart, the next anchorage or port, showing them the choice of locations in relation to the expected wind direction, where one might bring up on arrival. Similarly the choice of destination could be collectively made, pointing out the effect of wind and tide expected en route. This soon led to an appreciation of tidal streams, leeway, and how you have to aim off when laying a course to counteract them. And it was no time at all before our three could quickly and accurately recognise features on the land ahead from the representation on the chart, even when the area was totally new to them.

Using the hand bearing compass to establish our position was the next step, the achievement of a really small 'cocked hat' location on the chart being acclaimed with pride, as was a course which, worked out and then sailed, came to the right place. The miracle of that always remains a thrill.

Responsible solo watch-keeping

Now that an age has been reached where full night watches can be allowed, being left in sole charge of the deck for considerable periods can be tried, after suitable training (albeit with an adult on stand-by down below, at least first). The young helmsman must obviously be fully aware of the need to keep taking careful looks all round the horizon, and be able to judge accurately by the relative bearings of their lights, if any other vessels in the vicinity might be on a potential collision course with the yacht.

The fascination of steering a compass course over the darkened sea will soon take root. One very soon discovers which of the crew tends to steer slightly to which side of the course ordered (very few of us manage to go slap down the middle), and any youngster who knows his parents' little ways to this extent will derive endless satisfaction – as will any good navigator – from allowing for this knowledge when laying off a course for them to steer.

Compass-steering knacks, such as never staring fixedly at the binnacle for too long at a time, should be taught from the start. There is that inevitable tendency at night or in bad visibility with no horizon in view, to glue one's eyes to the swinging card, and so become mesmerised into a state of not knowing whether you're coming or going. More than once, with a learner at the helm, our own little ship has been blithely sailed in the diametrically opposite direction to the course ordered, with the watch-keeper totally unaware of his error – until the skipper came up and found out! ('So *that's* what's wrong . . . I thought the *wind* had changed!')

Handling warps

With growing strength, of course, come all the other abilities – if properly taught – such as warp handling. Throwing a warp in particular requires a surprising amount of skill, but is easily learned. Show the youngster how to divide the coil between his two hands, then throw the rope with a curving sweep of a straight arm, aiming the coil for the *body* of the person waiting to catch it, rather than towards his outstretched hand. (As the coil unwinds, it tends to curve through the air.)

Handling warps and fenders (and securing both items quickly and firmly) is one of the most useful accomplishments which one's family crew can attain, whether cruising coastwise or inland. Other people may be watching, or possibly wanting your crew to catch their warps and make them fast, so if it can be smartly done, everyone will feel pleased.

A real family crew

Not long after the two of us were first married, and before we had been able to raise our own crew, we had occasion to be caught out in the middle of a rather exposed West Highland harbour, at night, with a rapidly rising gale. As we worked feverishly to get our anchor and run in alongside in the lee of the tiny pier, a large cutter which had been lying close ahead of us came sweeping by, her oilskinned skipper shouting for us to come in and lie alongside her as soon as she was settled.

This we were very glad to do, for we knew the ancient timbers of the pier were extremely rough, and in the swell already finding its way in, we would have a much easier night of it strapped tightly to our neighbour than if we were ranging to and fro tearing our fenders to pieces and jerking on our warps. He clearly had spars and other gear available to take the wear, and it was a kind and very generous offer, in the circumstances.

As we came in, the skipper of the cutter turned on his deck

and spreader lights for us, and we could see his entire family ranged along the rail ready to catch us, and help make fast. It was only when we watched him attempt to secure one of our warps to a deck-cleat that we began to doubt the wisdom of so rapidly accepting the skipper's invitation, for even as he stepped away from it, we could see our rope working itself free!

Just then, a small shadow, oilskinned and lifejacketed, moved in its father's wake, smartly untied the rest of the knot completely – and did it up properly. With a glinting, twelve-year-old wink across to us, the glistening little figure moved on along the cutter's sidedeck, once more following in father's footsteps, to see that all the remaining warps 'secured' by his august parent were similarly checked and corrected. Clearly a normal part of that ship's procedure!

They turned out to be a very charming and close-knit family, with the sea flowing in the blood of every one of them, for when daylight came, after a noisy but none-the-less secure night, we arrived on deck to see that same young figure at the foot of their fifty-foot mast, hoisting the burgee of the 'Ocean Cruising Club'.

As much as anything else, that incident made us look forward keenly to the day when offspring of our own making might be able to rally round and help in a similar manner, perhaps returning the favour for someone else who would be glad of it.

And so it came to pass, for we eventually went to live near the Crinan Canal in Argyllshire, where our daughters became well-known figures as they took the warps and helped other yachts (as well as our own) through the locks and out towards the waters of the Hebrides.

HAPPY CRUISING!

INDEX